Gifts from Your Garden

Gifts from Your Garden

*A SEASONAL ALBUM OF
DECORATIONS AND KEEPSAKES*

Suzanne Frutig Bales

PRENTICE HALL GARDENING

New York   London   Toronto   Sydney   Tokyo   Singapore

PRENTICE HALL GENERAL REFERENCE
15 Columbus Circle
New York, NY 10023

Library of Congress Cataloging-in-Publication Data

Bales, Suzanne Frutig.
    Gifts from Your Garden / Suzanne Frutig Bales.
        p.   cm.
    Includes bibliographical references and index.
    ISBN 0-13-356155-0 :
    1. Flower arrangement.   2. Gardening.   3. Flowers—Utilization.
4. Cookery (Flowers)   5. Gifts.   I. Title.
SB449.B245   1992
745.92—dc20   91-43976
                                                                   CIP

Book designed by Barbara Cohen Aronica and Jan Halper Scaglia.
Manufactured in the United States of America

10   9   8   7   6   5   4   3   2   1
First Edition

DESIGN CREDITS FOR GIFTS FROM YOUR GARDEN
Suzanne Bales pages xiv, 3, 5, 7, 8, 10, 14, 15, 17, 20, 21, 22, 23, 25, 26, 28, 33, 39, 40, 41, 44, 46, 49, 50, 52 bottom, 54, 55, 58, 59, 60, 62, 63, 65, 67, 69, 72, 76, 77, 79, 81 top and bottom, 82, 84, 87, 88, 94, 95, 96, 99, 101, 107, 111, 112, 114, 115, 116, 124, 126, 129, 130, 132, 133, 135, 136, 138, 140 bottom, 414 top, 146, 148, 150, 155, 164, 169, 176, 187
Connie Cross, page 157
J. Barry Ferguson, pages x, 12, 13, 36, 52 top, 53, 91, 103, 152, 170, 179, 181
Gina Norgard, pages 25, 43, 81 middle
Peter Stevens, pages 15, 120, 139, 140 top, 143
Georgia Wall, pages 121, 141 bottom
Joan Williams, page 108
Martha Kraska, pages 123, 127

Photography credits:
By the author except where listed below
Elizabeth Billhardt, page 103
Ken Druse, cover photo and pages ii, 58, 63, 76, 77, 79, 117, 129, 130 top, 133, 146, 150, 164
Aaron Rezny, pages x, 12, 18, 120, 178, 179, 180, 181

For my mother,
Dorothy Johnson Frutig,
who shared her love of making things
with my sister, Jayne Mengel, and me.

ACKNOWLEDGMENTS

As in all endeavors, no one really works alone. All of the ideas in this book evolved from other projects I have seen and the influence of very talented designers and gardeners. J. Barry Ferguson has stood out as an individual whose enthusiasm for flowers and flower design spills over as he freely teaches others. I have been fortunate to have him as a friend and neighbor. Peter Stevens, who assisted Barry for many years, has also been generous with his designs and knowledge. Ken Druse, a noted garden writer and photographer, and his assistant Victor Nelson shared their knowledge and added their style to many of the designs they photographed for this book. Ruth Shapiro, a close friend and mentor, was very generous with her time, and was very encouraging during the early stages of this book. Ruth styled many of the pictures photographed by Aaron Rezny in his studio for W. Atlee Burpee & Co. Aaron's photography and keen eye have added much to this book. Elizabeth Billhardt, a long-time friend and creative photographer, also photographed several pictures.

Many people allowed me to photograph at their homes. I would like to thank Connie and Jim Cross, Reba and Dave Williams, Jack and Joan Williams, Martha and Peter Kraska, and Georgia Wall and Don Gogel.

In addition, my husband and dearest friend, Carter F. Bales, was very supportive of this book and all of the messes around the house I made in the process. My close friends, Martha Kraska, an expert gardener, and Gina Norgard, an accomplished chef, gave tons of advice and were always willing to help set up a shot or clean up a

Acknowledgments

mess. My children Tom, Margaret, Carter and Cathryn should be mentioned, even though at times they believed me to be a little wacky and loved to make jokes at my expense. They did, however, cajole me out of adding some of my more ridiculous creations.

Again, as in my other books, I have to thank my father who graciously gave freely of his time to edit and help me shape the book.

The team at Prentice Hall Gardening worked their magic once again. Rebecca Atwater edited and fine-tuned the manuscript, while Rachel Simon proofread and proofread again. I'm convinced nothing could get by their keen eyes. It was a pleasure to work with Lee Wade and Lori Singer as they designed the cover.

CONTENTS

A wooden Chinese bucket holds garden and roadside flowers arranged by J. Barry Ferguson. Included in the arrangement are Queen Anne's lace, snapdragons, lilies, Shasta daisies, delphiniums, lilacs and bachelor's buttons.

For a time, I was a closet gardener. Friends would call to invite me to play tennis, swim or come for lunch. In the beginning, I tried to tell the truth. "I'd love to, but I have some things I planned to do in my garden." The response was always the same. They felt gardening was a chore, and it was all but impossible to make them understand that I really loved gardening. But gardening was, and is, my favorite sport and recreation. So like most addicts, I took to making excuses when friends extended invitations, and I became a closet gardener, admitting the truth only when caught with dirty hands and broken fingernails.

But as my garden grew and improved, my friends' attitudes began to change. Tennis players and luncheon hostesses alike started coming to admire and pick the flowers, even seeking advice for their own gardens. Gardening is a love that keeps growing, a love that gardeners have to share with others. Giving gifts from your garden spreads the joy of gardening to others and illustrates the truth that "to create a garden is to make a better world."

A garden is a world of limitless imagination, a place for reflection amid beauty, a place of calm where you can closely observe nature. A garden endlessly unfolds its beauty. Flowers, depending on their personality and character, give of themselves and often become lifelong friends. Even the most mundane of garden chores brings you close to the ever-changing seasons, and you see the beauty in the passing storms, the coming and going of perennials, and the cooling of light rains as they bathe and cleanse the earth.

The garden and its wonders get us outside ourselves, our daily routines, even our troubles. Everyone has times of spiritual lows, and a garden, its growth, its change and the miracle of a larger power at work, puts our petty problems in their place. Time spent in the garden lightens your load as it puts your emotions in perspective and opens a world of natural beauty. Mother Nature—the irrepressible optimist—cheers, inspires and rejuvenates. She even entertains us with the songs of birds, the dances of butterflies and hummingbirds and the gymnastics of toads and praying mantises.

Within this book are simple ideas, easily adapted to a busy life-style, to help you enjoy your garden fully and share its gifts with friends and neighbors. Some of the most ingenious ideas are centuries old, for example, carrying a fragrant flower in your pocket for a natural perfume, decorating a table with rose petals or leaving an anonymous basket of flowers on a friend's doorstep. In the pages that follow I hope you find many new ideas as well as fresh twists on old ideas to encourage or rekindle a love of flowers. Borrow freely; an idea that's borrowed changes, improves and takes on some of the borrower's personality. It's all been done before but never quite the same way, just as the same recipe prepared by different people will yield a variety of results.

Let the joy of gardening and the gifts of the garden carry you happily through all the seasons. Even if you don't have a garden, don't despair. Most of the flowers and vegetables I use can be purchased from florists or grocery markets, or collected along the roadside. And certainly every flower or vegetable suggested can be switched beautifully with almost any other. I think of flowers the way most people think of money: There's never enough.

CHAPTER ONE

Spring

Crocuses and snowdrops are the first flowers to bloom—
reassuring the gardener that spring is on its way.

"In all places, then, in all seasons,
Flowers expand their light and soul-like wings,
Teaching us, by most persuasive reasons,
How akin they are to human things."
—*Longfellow*

Spring is a capricious seductress, beckoning and taunting us. Her warming trends invite us out, coax us into taking off our jackets, then our sweaters; and just as we believe she is here to stay, she vents her wrath, thundering with stormy tantrums. Or she plays the ultimate April Fool's trick, with temperature drops and blizzards, hiding and bending the daffodils in mounds of snow. Fortunately Mother Nature, our protectress and fairy godmother, has given spring flowers an amazing ability to cope, survive and shine through it all. Fortunately, too, a little of the flowers' optimism rubs off on the gardener, who knows that eventually spring showers will indeed bring summer's flowers.

Changeable spring weather creates conflicting feelings. It is the season we most want to rush, hurrying along the rains and mud, but it's also the season we want to linger, extending the life of ephemeral blooms by gathering spring beauties to bring inside for bouquets. And just when we tire of the changeable weather of spring and long for the even, predictable days of summer, capricious spring fools us again, prematurely exhaling a hot summery breath and rushing what we least want: the short bloom of the peony and even shorter bloom of the iris. Both fold and wilt under the glaring gaze of the unrelenting sun. Even cool nights won't save them. Mother

The few weeks when daffodils and tulips bloom together provide spectacular bouquets. Bulbs are inexpensive and can be planted every fall for a gift to yourself of spring bouquets. Tulips and daffodils have been bred with such abundance that many no longer resemble their ancestors. In the front of this arrangement are double-flowering tulips (the pink doubles are 'Angelique' and the white are 'Mount Tacoma'), looking more like peonies than tulips. Behind them are bright scarlet lily-flowering tulips and the small-cupped and trumpet daffodils. Purple lilacs and white mock-orange branches lend their beauty and fragrance to complete the arrangement.

Nature's gift to us of a peony, easily living a hundred years without much fuss or many demands, is certainly something to be grateful for—a plant to tip your hat to. Spread the news! A peony, when given as a gift, wishes longevity and brings smiles for a lifetime with its easy temperament. I attempt to hedge my bets against spring's withering glares by planting a mixture of varieties that bloom early, mid- and late season. Iris are not so accommodating, and some have bloomed and are gone in a day or two, but what a spectacular glimpse. It's good to be reminded of how temporary beauty can be; that is, if one's heart can stand it.

Even so, a walk in the spring garden will chase away the winter doldrums. How can you help but smile when greeted by the gnomelike faces of pansies, so full of mischief? Perhaps you don't approve of their families' frequency of intermarriage and shameless production of offspring that only vaguely resemble their parents and never result in identical twins. But, all things considered, it's easy to envy their jovial family, partying as they do through the wet and stormy weather of spring. Look a little closer at their innocent, brightly colored, intricately designed and expectant faces. Pluck a blossom or two to amuse yourself indoors. Take some to a friend to spread their happiness and say, in the language of flowers, "think of me."

Violets, the more reserved cousins, bloom sweetly at about the same time, fragrantly making their presence known while bashfully hiding their heads under heart-shaped leaves. Don't be fooled by their shyness and delicate fragrance. This family knows how to fend for itself. True, violets appear most fragile when first introduced into the garden. However, keep an eye on them. Once they form a community, they quietly stick together and send out spreading roots, tightly matted, which slowly and politely choke everything in their path. I do adore them, but I'm wary of their travels, and this gives me an excuse to dig the edges of the clump each spring and pot several to bring inside. I also pick many for nosegays and don't apologize for robbing the bed because they are not easily seen in the garden. The best way to show them off is to group the flowers in the center and surround them with a ring of heart-shaped leaves pointing outward. Tied with several very thin streamers of ribbons in various shades of purples and pinks, they are invited in and they are well-behaved, sharing their perfume and lasting a week or two. Violet flowers can also take in water through their petals. The bouquet can be submerged overnight to increase water intake, to refresh the flowers and help them last longer indoors.

Violets, though aggressive in the garden, have a quiet beauty and fragrance when brought inside.

During late winter or early spring the frozen ground thaws. I am drawn outdoors during the thaws and will dig a pot of snowdrops, violets, glory-of-the-snow or other small bulbs. They have never complained about being moved indoors quickly to a constant 68 degrees Fahrenheit, where they will stay in bloom for two weeks or longer. After suffering spring's abuse they are ready for a mild vacation, and when they have finished blooming I return all but the invasive violets to the garden, where they can die back, forming next year's flowers.

I'll always remember the first time I dug snowdrops. The earth was very wet and cold but easy to part with my trowel. I reached into the hole with bare hands, shunning gloves and their claustrophobic feel (as limiting as walking in the dark without a flashlight), to pull out gently the snowdrops' bulbs, root hairs and all. With my bare fingers I felt the roots and knew the outline of the plants as I led them out of the ground. Quickly I learned that poison-ivy roots are more potent in winter than their leaves in summer. I won't bore you with the blistering details, but caution you to wear gloves where poison-ivy roots are a possible encounter. At my house poison ivy is a foe I wrestle yearly, winning a few battles, but never the war.

DECORATIVE NESTS

The flowers signaling the coming of spring (snowdrops, crocuses and dwarf iris) are small and delicate. For a dinner table they can be combined with greens to create small garden scenes. Commemorate the return of the birds with a bird's nest, removed from a tree during winter when it is easier to spot and no one is home. If possible, take a small piece of the branch the nest rests on. That way the nest will look more at home as a spring centerpiece. There are also baskets commercially available that resemble birds' nests. Decorate the nest by intertwining it with ivy and filling it with wooden robin's eggs. Forsythia branches make an especially pretty setting for a nest; they can be laid directly on the table after conditioning and will last out of water.

A spring table commemorates the return of the birds, with forsythia branches cradling baskets shaped like birds' nests and filled with wooden eggs.

In March, when flowers are few, combine many small arrangements to give the dinner table a full look. The candle cup holds a mixture of evergreens including pines, leucothoe, Japanese euonymus, blue spruce and mountain laurel. Individual miniature bottles show off single dwarf iris blooms. Miniature china baskets are planted with babies' tears and have snowdrops and Siberian squill poked in. The bird-nest baskets are filled with wooden eggs and surrounded by variegated and plain, small-leaved ivy.

Later, when spring is in full swing and there is more to choose from, create bouquets of spring flowers to be viewed up close. Virginia bluebells, lungwort, and the delicate bleeding hearts, all blooming together outside, complement each other inside. As the season progresses bouquets can be made larger and more varied in composition.

MINIATURE ARRANGEMENTS

A gardening friend, Janet Hester, brings miniature flower arrangements to friends when she visits. At first glance I didn't recognize the flowers in the miniature basket she gave me (two by four inches with a small handle). The whole basket held only five flowers, but they looked different on two-inch stems than on the three-foot stems they stand on in the garden. She had used *Achillea* 'Moonbeam', which can have flowers four or more inches across, but she had broken the flower into individual bracts only an inch across.

I now keep miniature baskets in my gardener's cupboard, which allows me to make attractive small arrangements quickly and impulsively. The baskets are lined with aluminum foil and fitted with small pieces of floral foam. The handles can be decorated with ribbons or left plain. If made up of everlastings, a miniature basket can decorate an end table, bookcase or bedside table all winter long.

English garden writer Beverly Nichols called his miniature bouquets "Lilliputian bunches of mixed flowers," and he used, among other things, shot glasses, saltcellars and inkwells. Anything that holds water will work for fresh flowers: shells, teacups, mugs, wineglasses, saltshakers, boxes and whatever you find while taking a closer look through your cupboards. If you are making miniature

Left: A miniature basket filled with three red astilbe plumes, one blue salvia flower and four columbine blossoms.

Right: Queen Anne's lace, a roadside flower, and love-in-a-mist, a quick-blooming garden flower grown from seed, combine for an old-fashioned miniature arrangement.

arrangements with dried flowers the container doesn't need to hold water and can be fashioned from nearly anything, including cloth and paper bags, matchboxes and decorative cardboard or papier-mâché boxes.

CANDLE CUPS

Aluminum candle cups, designed to hold arrangements of flowers at the base of candle holders, are particularly useful when there are few flowers available, small flowers with short stems or even large flowers such as tulips that have broken off from their stems. If space is limited on the dining table, candle cups are ideal because they take up only the space at the base of the candle holder or candelabrum, permitting guests to see each other across the table. An arrangement can be rustic or elegant depending on whether you use a wooden candle holder, or a glass, crystal or silver one. J. Barry Ferguson, who introduced me to candle cups, recommends trailing a vine such as jasmine, small-leaved ivy or honeysuckle on a tall candlestick for its softening effect. With a large, branching candelabrum he recommends using just one central candle cup and surrounding it with candles.

The candle cup is first fitted with floral foam shaped into a half sphere. You can visualize the shape by thinking of a scoop of ice cream fitting into a cone. The floral foam is soaked in water for a minimum of an hour before it is taped in place, inside the candle cup, using green floral tape. If the cup wobbles in the candle holder, floral clay will hold it in place. The candle is then pushed gently into the top of the floral foam and the flowers and greens can be added. Taller candles work better; 18-inch tapers will burn longer and keep the flames out of your guests' eyes. It is best to start with the greens and the trailing plants to hide the aluminum cup before adding the flowers that reach up and out. Be sure to keep the flowers away from where the flame will be both at the beginning and end of the evening.

Left: A formal arrangement of yellow roses and variegated ivy spills from a candle cup in the center of a silver candelabrum.

Right: The candle cup is fitted with floral foam, like a scoop of ice cream in a cone. The "scoop" is taped in place, then the candle and flower are added. Pictured here are daffodils, hyacinths and ivy.

The small size of the candle cup makes it easy to keep the arrangement for a week or two if the floral foam is kept moist and cool by storing the candle cup in a plastic bag in a cool dark place such as the refrigerator. Just reattach the candle cup to the candlestick, replace the used candle and your arrangement is ready.

In spring candle cups can be covered with miniature daffodils and grape hyacinths, which bloom beautifully together whether they be inside or out. While arranging flowers for the house you may discover flowers that complement each other in an arrangement, and decide to plant them together in the garden.

SPRING WREATHS

Grapevines twisted into wreaths (easily made in fall or winter, or purchased from garden centers, craft shops or garden catalogs) can be decorated with spring flowers for greeting guests at the door or decorating the dinner table. Spring flowers generally need water, and floral tubes are perfect for this, hiding easily under the wreath or hidden with leaves and ribbons. Daffodils and Virginia bluebells (*Mertensia*) not only bloom beautifully when planted together in the garden but complement each other in a spring grapevine wreath. Even shrubs such as lilac and flowering almond can twist through a grapevine base for a fragrant, spring wreath.

A wreath can be special and interesting year 'round, either hung on a door or laid flat as a centerpiece with a candle or a bowl of fruit in the center. A spring wreath can be made from less traditional plants for flower arranging such as groundcovers, flowering shrubs and flowering trees. It can be a dramatic centerpiece, easily made even when there are few flowers in the cutting garden.

Grapevines are twisted into wreaths that can be saved and reused with each season. This spring wreath is filled with lilacs and flowering quince.

A spring floral-foam wreath is covered with the green leaves of pachy-sandra and decorated with the blue flowers of ajuga, pink flowers of azalea and white flowers of dogwood.

A set of foam rings purchased from a floral-supply store will enable you to make beautiful arrangements without much effort. Soak a ring for an hour in warm water while you pick the flowers. Cut the stems of the greens and the flowers on a slant to allow them to take up water more easily (see page 174 for how to condition flowers for longer life). Cover the ring with short-

This topiary rabbit, planted with small-leaved ivy by designer Peter Stevens, lives in the garden year 'round. He is a source of much fun for our family. At times I've found him holding a squirt gun, a doll and even a basket of withered flowers. At Easter, of course, a basket of tinted eggs is obligatory. Mother Nature shows her interest in our rabbit by dressing him appropriately to greet each season. Spring brings new light green leaves, summer a necklace of white clematis, autumn a colorful hat of fallen leaves, and winter turns him into a snow bunny. Occasionally the children dress the snow bunny with a carrot, a scarf and a hat.

stemmed pachysandra, starting with the inside circle and covering the top and outer edge completely, keeping the leaves flat against the ring. I use pachysandra as a green canvas on which to splatter color. It is so readily available, rarely bothered by slugs and chewing insects, and most of the time the leaves are a perfect dark green. Flowers stand out nicely against this background. After the wreath is completely covered with pachysandra and no floral foam is visible, I add the flowers of ajuga, pink azalea and dogwood. Gently press the stems of the flowers into the floral foam until you feel resistance. Gently, because if you jam them in you will break the stems and have less to work with. The wreath can be hung on the door to greet guests, an unexpected pleasure in the spring, or used as a centerpiece complete with a votive candle as pictured, or with a more elegant tall candle and glass hurricane lantern. If the wreath is used on a table it is best to place it on a shallow, round dish like a dinner plate to enable you to keep it in a reservoir of water. A glass plate won't distract from the arrangement.

POTS OF PRIMROSES

The brilliant jewel tones of primroses, which flower for many weeks in the spring, bring out the greed in my soul. I never seem to have enough of them in the garden. But where I want them most is indoors, to brighten up the house. Primroses are not, as their name might imply, prim and proper or stiff and staid. They aim to please. They give generously of their blooms, and just when you think they might be finished, they could decide to send up another round of buds. Each spring I buy a pot or two (or three) and put them in

A pot of primroses pops out of a wooden box. The soil and plastic container are hidden with Spanish moss.

the house to enjoy for a week or more until the hot, dry air gets them down. At this point, I plant them in the garden, where they revive with the cool nights and continue to bloom for weeks more. One way to display them inside is popping, jack-in-the-box style, out of a wooden box. Spanish moss hides their soil and the rim of their plastic pots.

FLORAL FOAM

When floral foam is purchased in rings for making wreaths, the set includes three concentric rings and the "hole" from the center. Each floral foam form has a plastic tray on the bottom, eliminating the need for a base. The "hole" makes an interesting centerpiece, looking like an island planting when it is covered with ivy and decorated with daffodils. This is a perfect imitation of the way daffodils look best in the landscape. Pachysandra and myrtle combine equally well with daffodils, whether inside in arrangements or outside in the garden.

An island of ivy and daffodils made from the "hole" of floral foam in a set of floral-foam rings.

POT UP EXTRA SEEDLINGS

In spring when planting flats of annuals and vegetables or dividing perennials or herbs, put a few aside and plant them individually in pots or baskets for friends. It won't be long before they grow and bloom and you'll have wonderful gifts waiting for distribution. Later, several small pots can be combined in a basket or bowl, the soil and the pot rims hidden with Spanish or green moss, the way they are displayed in many florists' shops. Or several herbs can be combined in a wooden box or pot for a container garden and placed by a friend's kitchen door.

CELEBRATIONS OF SPRING

With today's overcrowded cities, air and water pollution and the destruction of rain forests, it's hard to imagine that in the middle of the last century, a warning came from J. Sterling Mortin, a Nebraska resident, angry at the wanton clearing and desecration of the western plains by settlers. He organized an annual planting contest where prizes were awarded to the clubs and granges that planted the most trees. He was so successful that April 22, 1872, marked the first Arbor Day with one million trees planted across Nebraska's barren prairies. A century later, Arbor Day is still celebrated across America, but halfheartedly at best.

A bouquet of flowers can be left on a friend's doorstep to celebrate May Day. This bouquet is made up of tulips, daffodils, snowflakes and Virginia bluebells.

A gift of a tree or a shrub, planted in memory of a friend, a birth, a wedding, or a graduation, is a lasting memory and a gift returned to Mother Earth.

May Day is a very old holiday few of us remember and even fewer of us celebrate. May Day is May first, and the custom, years ago, was to ring the doorbell of a special friend, leave a basket of flowers and run away without being seen. Create a bouquet yourself and leave it on a friend's doorstep on May first (or any day). The act itself expresses your love. Compose a note using the language of flowers as your guide (see page 163).

SPRING IN FULL SWING

From mid- to late spring the garden is an explosion of bloom. This is a time to experiment with arrangements combining branches of flowering shrubs, vines and bulbs. Simple arrangements, quickly gathered and bunched, need only be planned for complementary color. The colors of the vase can also be coordinated with the arrangement.

Flowering almond, 'Angelique' tulips and flowering pear branches make this watering can quite elegant.

Lily-flowering tulips, red Darwin hybrid tulips and double-flowered white tulips are held in place by an inexpensive string of pearls (the sort sold as Christmas tree decorations).

The quiet colors of Greenland tulips, purple wisterias, lilacs, checkered lilies, white daffodils and white bells of Solomon's seal make a lovely combination.

Lettuce from the garden can be a whimsical centerpiece.

EDIBLE FLOWERS

Flowers have been considered food by many cultures for centuries. The Japanese cook daylily buds, the Italians fry zucchini blossoms and the French make rose-flavored desserts. Always check whether a flower is indeed edible before tasting it, and never eat sprayed flowers. Many flowers can be used in a multitude of ways—adding color to salads, decorating a pat of butter, floating in drinks. Some flowers such as tulips and zucchini blossoms are large enough to stuff with chicken or other main-course salads. Others are used for flavorings in herbal teas, liqueurs, vinegars, sorbets, custards, butters, soups and sauces. Add flowers as flavorings to tea, vinegar or vodka. Mix one cup of best-quality loose tea with one to two tablespoons dried (unsprayed) petals of roses, marigolds or jasmine. Fill a bottle of wine vinegar with borage or chive flowers. Substitute rose water for vanilla flavoring in icings and fillings. A violet liqueur is made by steeping two cups of vodka with forty heads of scented violets, one cup of granulated sugar and a small piece of vanilla bean.

Before cooking with a flower, taste it to see if you like its flavor. Flowers with a strong scent like lavender may be overpowering and should be used sparingly. There are hundreds of varieties of marigolds that are very spicy and taste rather awful. Rosalind Creasy, an American expert on edible flowers and author of *Cooking from the Garden*, suffered through many samples to find the best ones and she recommends the Climax series, 'Lemon Gem', and 'White Snowbird' marigolds. Marigold petals dry easily and can be stored in an airtight jar for winter use in cakes, breads and muffins. The petals of some flowers including roses, pot marigolds, chrysanthemums and lavender, have a white base that is bitter and should be removed.

Leaves and herbs make an attractive bed for cheese or an hors d'oeuvre. My favorites are Swiss chard with its beautiful red leaves,

Left: Flowers are painted with egg white and sprinkled with superfine sugar to make candied-flower decorations that will last for many months.

A candied pansy and many candied violets and scented geranium flowers decorate a chocolate torte.

purple basil for deep purple color, green or variegated nasturtium leaves for their round lily-pad shape and red cabbage for its silvery gray-blue leaves.

Candied Flowers

Many flowers can be candied and used as tasty snacks or to decorate desserts. This is a practice that was common in 17th- and 18th-century Europe. The flowers that work best are violets, Johnny-jump-ups, scented geraniums, pansies and roses. This process was taught to me by Rosalind Creasy, and is so simple that it is also a good activity to do with children. All you need is a gently beaten egg white, a small paintbrush and superfine sugar. Wash the flowers gently in cool running water, pat dry, paint with egg white on both sides and sprinkle with superfine sugar. The flowers must be completely covered with egg white and sugar. The egg white and sugar act as a preservative and the color and shape will last for months or even a year if stored properly. Allow them to dry and harden in a colander or on a clean screen where there is good air circulation and low humidity. When dry the blossoms will be hard and easy to move. Store in a sealed jar.

Any edible flowers make good fritters, but the sweeter-tasting flowers such as rose petals and violets are the most popular. Apples or bananas can be combined with the flowers for variation. Here, rose-petal fritters are decorated with powdered sugar and fresh rose petals.

FLOWER FRITTERS

1⅓ cups all-purpose flour
1 tablespoon vegetable oil
¾ cup beer
2 tablespoons granulated sugar
2 egg yolks, beaten
¾ cup edible flower petals
Confectioners' sugar
Vegetable oil for deep-fat frying
2 egg whites

Combine the first five ingredients in a bowl, mix well and let sit for at least three hours before deep frying. (The batter can keep overnight if covered and stored in the refrigerator. It should be brought to room temperature before the fritters are fried.)

Wash the flower petals with lukewarm water and pat dry on paper towels. Sprinkle the dried petals on both sides with confectioners' sugar.

Heat the vegetable oil at least two inches deep in a saucepan or deep-fat fryer. The oil is ready when a drop of water sprinkled on top sizzles. While the oil is heating beat the egg whites until stiff and fold them into the batter. Next fold the flower petals into the batter. (Sliced bananas and apples can also be added at this time.) Drop a tablespoon of batter into the hot oil. If it sizzles and swells the oil is the perfect temperature. Continue to add tablespoons of fritter batter one at a time until the pan is full but the fritters are not touching each other. Fry to a golden brown on all sides. Remove the fritters with a slotted spoon and drain them on paper towels. Sprinkle with confectioners' sugar and they are ready to serve.

Blooming Salad

Flowers in modern times have been used as a beautiful garnish for salads and other foods, but they are again, as in times past, appearing in dishes for their flavor as well as their beauty. While some flowers are similar to lettuce in not really having much flavor, many are very flavorful. The flowers of borage have a strong cucumber flavor, chive flowers add an onion flavor, bee balm has a minty

A flower salad features pansies, scented geraniums, pot marigold petals, rose petals, chive petals, nasturtiums, thyme, Johnny-jump-ups, borage and violets.

lemon flavor, lemon thyme has the pungency and flavor of lemon, pot marigold flowers are tangy, tuberous begonias have a light lemon flavor, honeysuckle tastes like honey and pinks have a spicy clovelike flavor. Lavender is very pungent and should be added in small doses. Nasturtiums have beautiful flowers with little flavor, but their leaves are very spicy and can be substituted for ground pepper. Tulips have a crisp texture and are similar to peas in flavor but a little sweeter. (Make sure you remove the pollen and stigma from tulips before using; they don't taste good.) Violets, apple blossoms, lilacs and roses have a sweet floral taste, but here too, each variety has a slightly different flavor. This means you must smell and taste the flower before you use it to avoid disappointment. The best-tasting flowers are usually the most fragrant. The more fragrant the flower, the stronger the flavor; use with discretion. Some edible flowers such as calendulas, chives, lavender and roses have hard centers that are not tasty. In these cases use only the petals, not the whole flower.

Rose Flavoring

Cooking with rose petals is an art that has been passed from generation to generation for centuries. Here again, the more fragrant the petals, the more flavorful they are. 'Don Juan' is a very fragrant climbing red rose and especially good for flavoring. Most roses have a sweet floral flavor, but some, *Rosa rugosa*, for example, are more clovelike than sweet. Taste before you cook. Rose petals should be picked fresh in the morning when they are the plumpest before the sun dries them out. Rose water (see page 31) can be used to flavor custards, cakes, ice creams and other desserts in the same way vanilla flavoring is used. Rose-flavored sugar can be substituted for plain sugar to flavor desserts.

Rose Sugar

Rose sugar is easy to make. Wash the individual rose petals in lukewarm water, pat dry with towels and then trim off the white inside tip of the petal (because it can be bitter). Allow the roses to dry thoroughly on a screen before alternating a layer of petals with a thin covering of sugar in a clean glass jar. Cover the jar tightly and set aside for a few hours or overnight in a cool, dry place. The sugar will absorb the oil and essence of the rose petals' fragrance. Later pour the sugar and rose petals through a sieve to remove the rose petals before they start to shrivel. The rose-flavored sugar can be stored in the same jar.

GINA'S ROSE CUSTARD

4 egg yolks
½ cup Rose Sugar (above)
1 cup heavy cream
1 cup milk
1 teaspoon red Rose Water (page 31) or 1 teaspoon vanilla

Whisk the egg yolks with the rose sugar over low heat in a saucepan. As the mixture thickens, slowly add the heavy cream and milk in a steady stream, whisking constantly. Heat almost to boiling. Let cool and add the rose or vanilla flavoring. If you use red Rose Water, the custard will have a pink cast. Refrigerate the custard until ready to serve. Serves 4.

ROSE WATER

1 cup water
1 cup fragrant pink and/or red rose petals

Bring the water and rose petals to a boil. Boil for one minute, cover and let cool. By the time the water is cool, the petals will have tinted the water rosy. (White and yellow roses can be used but you won't have the rosy color.) Strain the liquid through a sieve into a decorative bottle and discard the petals.

Depending on its concentration, rose water is used as a toilet water, added to a bath, as an astringent to splash on the face after washing in the morning, or as a flavoring for custards and cakes. It makes a nice gift for friends. It is easy to make, but lasts only a few days.

ROSE PASTE

1 cup (packed) rose petals
1 tablespoon salt

Combine the rose petals and salt in a food processor or blender for a few seconds until the mixture forms a paste. Place in a tightly sealed ceramic jar. (A glass jar may be used if it is kept away from light; for this reason, ceramic is more convenient.) As the mixture sits, the salt will release the oil from the petals and make a strong fragrance. This fragrance will keep indefinitely, as salt is a preservative. Remove the cover to add fragrance to a room.

FLOWERS IN ICE

Individual flowers frozen in ice cubes can make a drink sparkle and shine. (Make sure you use only edible flowers.) Wash the flowers with lukewarm water and place each blossom in an individual ice-cube compartment that is half full of water. Flowers float, so if you want the flower to be in the middle of the cube, it has to be frozen first in a half-filled tray; add more water later to form the top half of the cube.

For special occasions, you can use flowers to decorate an ice sculpture in the shape of a bucket to hold a wine or champagne bottle. The same procedure, adding water and more flowers as the sculpture freezes, must be followed. A small plastic bucket can be used to shape the ice sculpture. Place a smaller bucket inside the first bucket to form a hollow center. Fill the small bucket with weights (rocks or frozen food will work) to keep the bucket from floating as water is added around it. Depending on the size of the finished ice bucket, water and flowers can be added in three or four stages. Arrange the flowers randomly around the bucket—the more the merrier. Ferns and other foliage can be added for an even more colorful effect.

A quicker method will produce an interesting crackled effect. Pile ice cubes and blossoms to the top of the space between the two buckets. The cubes will hold the flowers down when water is added to fill in the cracks. Place buckets in the freezer for six hours or until frozen solid.

To unmold, turn the bucket upside down in the sink and run warm water on the bottom of the plastic bucket until it releases the ice bucket. The inside bucket can then be filled with warm water and allowed to sit for a few minutes until it is also released. Return

Edible flowers frozen in ice cubes are a pretty addition to any drink.

the ice sculpture to the freezer on a tray until needed or use it immediately.

Caution: Some flowers are poisonous—potato, foxglove and sweet pea, to name a few. Make sure you know which ones are harmless. The following flowers are edible, provided they haven't been sprayed with harmful pesticides:

EDIBLE FLOWERS

Common name	Latin name
Bee balm	*Monarda* species
Cornflower	*Centaurea cyanus*
Daylily	*Hemerocallis* species
Hollyhock	*Alcea rosea*
Honeysuckle	*Lonicera japonica*
Jasmine	*Jasminum* species
Johnny-jump-up	*Viola tricolor*
Lilac	*Syringa vulgaris*
Marigold	*Tagetes* species
Nasturtium	*Tropaeolum* species
Pansy	*Viola* × *Wittrockiana*
Pink	*Dianthus*
Pot marigold	*Calendula* species
Rose	*Rosa* species
Scented geranium	*Pelargonium* species
Tuberous begonia	*Begonia* × *tuberhybrida*
Tulip	*Tulipa* species
Violet	*Viola cornuta*

Herb Flowers

Borage
Chive
Hyssop
Mustard blossom
Thyme

Edible Flowers from Vegetables and Fruits

Apple blossom
Broccoli flower
Pea blossom (not sweet-pea blossoms, which are poisonous)
Plum blossom
Scarlet runner bean blossom
Squash and zucchini blossoms
Strawberry blossom

CHAPTER TWO

Summer

Celebrate the abundance of summer flowers with a party
in the garden.

"Blest childhood's darling, the Buttercup,
With bright rays gilt, as its flowers glance up."
—*Twamley*

Summer, when flowers are plentiful, is the season to consider any excuse for a celebration. What better time to entertain friends than when the garden is a kaleidoscope of colors? As the days lengthen, an early evening party will show your garden at its best. In the warm light of late afternoon, guests are drawn to the garden's edge by the vivid colors that glow in the radiance of the setting sun.

THE GARDEN PARTY

Garlands add the romance of a bygone era to a summer party. They are traditionally made at Christmas with evergreens, but in summer, garlands of flowering vines can be hung over a door, draped over a table or around a skirted tablecloth. They gracefully evoke a mood of romance and gentle pleasures. Vines make very festive party decorations. Any vine can be used if conditioned first (see page 174) and then the stem put in a floral plastic tube. The simplest swag is attached in two places, a quarter of its length from each end, allowing the center to sway or gracefully drape down and

Left: Float a single flower in a birdbath to dress up the garden for a party.

Below: A long vine of sweet peas is pinned to a table skirt. The ribbon hides a plastic water tube that keeps the flowers fresh.

then back up. Garlands can be made with lengths of vine used singly or twisted together. Ivy, honeysuckle, clematis and perennial sweet pea all work well. Depending on how supple the vine is, twist or loosely braid three lengths of vine together. If the vine needs water to keep from wilting, the ends can be inserted in water tubes and the tubes hidden with ribbons, leaves or additional flowers. Small-flowered clematis vines and ivy will do fine out of water for six hours. They can be used to decorate a chandelier or pinned on the skirt of a buffet table, leaving the entire top free for food. Punch bowls or ice buckets become centerpieces themselves when vines are wrapped around their bases. Edible flowers can be frozen in ice cubes or a simple bouquet can be frozen in a block of ice to float in a punch bowl.

Honeysuckle has limp stems that can be braided for a full garland to drape around a table skirt. The garland is attached with straight pins.

A summer wreath on the garden gate is covered with pachysandra and decorated with ageratums, dahlias, Salvia patens, *zinnias, cosmos and butterfly snapdragons.*

An unexpected and welcome surprise to bring the mood of the party to the arriving guests is to greet friends by decorating your front yard, mailbox, garden gate, door or front deck with flowers. Dress up the garden for an occasion: Use your birdbath as a centerpiece and float flowers or petals in it. Virtually anything can be hung with summer wreaths or wrapped with flowering vines. The summer wreath in the picture above was decorated with dahlias, ageratums, salvias, cosmos and butterfly snapdragons.

PARTY CAKE

A birthday or party cake decorated with edible flowers and complete with a pond of swimming goldfish is a surprise for children and adults alike, the very creation of which can be a fun activity to get the birthday girl or boy involved. Bake the cake in a rectangular pan and cut out an area in the center to accommodate a small aluminum-foil pan. Cover the pan's floor with marbles or tiny white gravel and fill the pan with room-temperature tap water. If you'd like a blue pond, add a little blue food coloring to the water. Next frost the cake and decorate it with fresh, edible flowers. At the last minute, add fish purchased at the pet store to the pan. (After the party the fish join those in our pond or the kids' fish tank). From time to time I have used birthday cakes to celebrate adult friends' birthdays with a golf course, pool or garden theme, adding doll-house miniatures for accents.

LUNCH IN THE SHADE

In the hot days of summer it is more comfortable to have lunch outdoors at a table under a sun umbrella. The only question is where to put the flower arrangement. Hydrangeas provide the answer; they are one of God's special gifts because of their beauty, lasting on the tree or shrub for many months and keeping indoors all winter long with minimum care. For the design on page 44, I piled hydrangea blossoms on the table around the pole of the umbrella without even putting them in water. Lilies, also without water, were poked in and around the hydrangeas. Additional flowers were scattered on the tablecloth, including hollyhock, stock and cornflowers. Sweet-pea vines were twisted into napkin

My daughter Katy's party cake was decorated with dollhouse furniture, edible flowers (bachelor's buttons, marigolds and nasturtiums) and a miniature pond complete with live goldfish. It was a real hit! Katy's pet rabbit Chocolate Chip joined the party.

A close-up of these flowers reveals they're no worse off for being out of water.

rings. The hydrangeas and lilies looked good for three days, after which I moved the hydrangeas to my drying closet, where they faded to the color of old denim, to be used again indoors for dried arrangements in the fall. The lilies I tossed on the compost pile.

Vines would be lovely camouflage for an umbrella pole, or use them to decorate the scallops of the umbrella or weave a pattern inside, draping them gracefully over the spokes. Twinkling, battery-operated lights could be added for evening making a frivolous but intimate corner for a small dinner party. There are many other ways to decorate an umbrella pole. An assortment of tall, thin vases placed around the umbrella pole would allow flowers to encircle the pole. Garden stores also stock ready-made planters that fit together as they surround the pole.

A MINIATURE GARDEN AS A CENTERPIECE

For a party celebrating the birthday of a gardening friend, create a miniature tabletop garden. First glue sheets of oak moss to the outside and over the rim of a plastic box. Next set an oval glass bowl in one end for a miniature fish pond and fill the rest of the box half full with damp potting soil. In one corner, near the bowl, flat rocks on top of the soil resemble a terrace. The remaining soil is covered with a variety of small-leaved groundcovers from various parts of the garden, some in flower like creeping phlox and *Mazus reptans*, and others, added for their texture and small size, include Scotch moss, green moss, creeping thyme and the silver-leaved *Helichrysum petiolatum*. The dollhouse miniature furniture and garden utensils add interest and support the small-scale garden. The final touches are blue rocks (from a pet shop) and water to make the fish pond come alive. Real goldfish or plastic fish can be added to the miniature pond.

A miniature garden makes an unusual centerpiece. It can be given to a friend and replanted in her garden.

HOSTESS GIFTS

Summer is also a time for visiting friends. Any of these garden gifts will please your hostess or host:
Fresh or dried potpourri (page 73)
Basket of rose petals (page 71)
Herb vinegars (page 96)
Herb oils (page 97)
Bouquet garni (page 97)
Pot of flowers (page 19)
Bouquet in an unusual container (page 48)

DECORATING WITH SUMMER FLOWERS

Flowers can dress up anything from a haircomb to a dinner table. There are so many ways to use them that I never have enough. Of course, there is always the florist's shop to supplement my supply, but if you're lucky enough to live in or visit the country, roadside flowers are a way of extending your garden and adding interesting wildflowers to your bouquets. The rule to follow when gathering roadside flowers is to pick only one of ten flowers. It is important to leave flowers to go to seed and replenish the supply for next year. Many of our roadside flowers arrived with the early settlers and have escaped from the garden and naturalized, crowding out indigenous species. If the flowers you want are on your state's list of noxious weeds, you can pick as many as you like. Some of the most invasive and out-of-control roadside plants make wonderful cut flowers: Queen Anne's lace, purple loosestrife, joe-pye weed, golden rod and iron weed. (Golden rod is not the culprit that causes allergies. Its pollen is so heavy, it falls to the ground rather than floating in the air.). All are beautiful in arrangements and baskets and some can be hung to dry.

It's never too early in the summer to start harvesting flowers for drying. For me it is a weekly project to pick and hang a few bunches (see page 105). Toward the end of summer, I spend even more time gathering flowers for drying, and when frost is expected I become a whirling top, afraid I won't gather all the flowers I need. Luckily, in my Zone 7 garden, I can still pick a few blooming renegades in protected areas even after a frost.

Summer is the time when returning from the garden with armfuls of flowers is the norm. The old saying, "the more you give, the more you get," is certainly true for cut flowers. The more flowers you cut, the more flowers the plants produce. It's another example of Mother Nature's generosity, a way of helping us to help ourselves.

Picking and giving flowers to friends is what a garden is all about. Don't let the expense of containers stop you; be imaginative. Look again at the supermarket tin cans and jam jars we toss regularly into the garbage. Some of these make interesting, humorous and attractive containers for bouquets. If you are using glass jars and bottles, you can add a few drops of food coloring to the water to perk up the container without hurting the flowers. Cans can also be decorative when wrapped with wide ribbons, tied in bows with streamers hanging, and appropriate for either the country kitchen or the fanciest dinner party, depending on your choice of ribbons. For the adventuresome, a cascading plant or flower can be arranged in an old shoe or boot. Perhaps it's a birthday party and your note could say, "You're as comfortable, as easy to be with and as loved as an old shoe."

Color is the most important element in flower arrangements. When arranging flowers, play with the juxtaposition of blossoms— notice the contrasts. Often I discover two flowers next to each other in a vase, and I like the look so much that I'll rearrange the flowers in my garden, bringing the two together where they can

Recycled cans and jars make interesting flower vases, especially handy for taking flowers to friends. In the glass jars the water is colored (with food coloring) to coordinate with the color of the flowers.

A whimsical bouquet given in an old shoe says "Only you are as comfortable, as easy to be with and as loved as an old shoe."

complement each other. In the abundance of summer it is hard to limit your flower colors. If you group several flowers of the same kind or color together and place another pleasing flower group next to them, you can continue around your bouquet, adding a slash of blue here, a sweep of silver there, mix in a few scarlet patches with a wave of golden yellow, with perhaps a little purple slipped in between. You can get away with adding almost any color if you are careful about which colors touch. Remember, stronger, bolder flowers need fewer in their group to make an impact; delicate, softer ones need more.

> *"I still go on going against the rules. That*
> *is the only way one can learn."*
> —*V. Sackville-West,* A Joy of Gardening

When arranging your flowers, don't forget to add interesting foliage. Often colorful foliage by itself is enough to create a centerpiece. The brightly colored, even brassy, foliage of coleus looks right at home floating in a Japanese Imari bowl. In the evening, floating candles add sparkle and shine, reflecting on the water.

J. Barry Ferguson's arrangement captures the colors of sunlight with yellow and white sunflowers, foxtail lilies and white hybrid lilies.

Various shades of pink and red are complemented by the dashes of blue flowers in this end-of-summer bouquet. Flowers included are blue salvia, pink cosmos, blue spiky globe thistle, hardy begonia, Mexican sage, hollyhock and red miniature dahlia.

Hosta, our shady friend, can lend his large leaves to cradle and wrap a bouquet. Lamb's ears, like a soft gray cashmere sweater, adds a texture and feel all its own. Silvery artemisia and dusty miller can act as a buffer between warring colors, adding peace and elegance to arrangements. If you're still unsure of colors, look at your favorite fabric or wallpaper for combination ideas. Don't be afraid to experiment with a few bold combinations such as purple and orange. Try orange wallflowers with blue dame's rockets.

Tropical flowers, such as this protea from the florist, add an exotic look to the table when combined with roses in a Chinese wooden bucket.

Hosta leaves can be used to wrap a bouquet for a friend. This arrangement features dill, orange cosmos 'Bright Lights', blue larkspur, pink and white sweet peas and light pink pincushion flower.

The best arrangements enhance the room or table they decorate by using colors that complement the decor and by keeping their size in proportion to their surroundings. A miniature arrangement would be lost on a dinner table, but a grouping of miniature arrangements could create a delicate, romantic feeling. Conversely, a three-foot-high flower arrangement would dominate a dining table, hiding the guests. A large arrangement works best in an entrance hall, a corner or against a wall.

A collection of teapots, all with a garden theme, is dressed up with simple bouquets of yellow marigold and red cosmos.

FRAGRANT FLOWERS

"The lilac has a load of balm
For every wind that stirs."

—Willis

Give a fragrant nosegay (see page 75). See the lists of fragrant flowers on page 171 or try the lesser-known mignonette (Reseda odorata). Mignonette is French for "little darling," and its fragrance is its fortune if its appearance is not. Anyone who has breathed the fragrance of mignonette would certainly like to have a bouquet.

Each flower, like each person, has a story to tell—of its origins, its history, its family life—and in the course of telling will reveal its personality and character. Mignonette is a native of Egypt, where it was one of the flowers chosen to adorn the burial place of mummies. A high honor among flowers, but not a particularly interesting existence. Later, when it was used medicinally because it was thought to have a calming effect, the seeds were exported to France, where it showed up as a garden flower in the early 18th century. It became a favorite of the empress Josephine. As the story goes, Napoleon collected the seeds during his Egyptian campaign and sent them back to Josephine for her garden. She grew mignonette as a pot plant to bring its musky fragrance indoors. Its popularity increased and demand for it spread so that by the end of the 19th century it was to be found in almost every garden in France. In the south of France it was grown commercially to meet the demand for winter bouquets in Paris and other large cities.

The story will make you wonder how it came to be so overlooked today, unheard of, unsung, dropped from favor and out of sight. Is it because outward beauty is all-important and mignonette is not a particularly attractive flower? It can also be loved for its easy ways, blooming in dry, infertile soil and refusing to provide fragrance when pampered in a too-fertile garden. It is readily found in garden catalogs and easily grown from seed. Acquire some seeds and grow it to provide fragrant bouquets for your house. Perhaps its fame will return.

WEARABLE FLOWERS

When I was young, special occasions were marked by wearing a corsage. I remember my first wrist corsage—the event was a sixth-grade dance—and the ritual of pressing it into my scrapbook. Every Easter, dad gave my mother, my sister and me corsages of gardenias, which we wore all day and then left on the table next to our beds to enjoy the sweet fragrance for several more days, even though the flowers had turned brown.

Summer flowers can be worn on combs, hats, headbands and necklaces, and can be carried in nosegays.

A tiny hand-blown glass vase will keep a single rose or a small bouquet fresh and fragrant all day.

I have recently started wearing flowers again, only this time from my garden and without adornments of frilled netting or artificial coloring. Simple arrangements let the beauty of the flowers themselves shine through. If you keep some supplies on hand and understand which flowers last longest, it is a simple matter to add flowers to your dress or hat as you go out. I once used a bobby pin to hold a passionflower (*Passiflora caerulea*) in my hair when I went to a summer party. Its waxy petals last well out of water and the bright purple color and perfect shape fooled many people into believing I was wearing an artificial flower. Or maybe, unaccustomed to seeing people wearing real flowers, they just assumed it was plastic.

Flower pins are returning to gift and flower shops. They range in price from Two's Company's inexpensive hand-blown, tiny glass vase on a stickpin (pick a posy, wear it all day) to the Vermont Company's handcrafted silver vase pins to Tiffany & Co.'s gold pin that resembles the anthers of a flower and is meant to be pinned through the center of a flower. I have also noticed antique silver flower posy holders at flea markets and in old-jewelry stores. All of them are designed to trap an air bubble inside so even when they are turned upside down they won't drip unless shaken.

Here are some simple, quick and attractive ways to wear flowers:

Headbands, barrettes, combs and pins can be decorated with garden flowers in minutes. Plain barrettes, combs, bases for pins and unadorned headbands can be purchased at most dime stores and drugstores. The best way to attach flowers to the ornaments is by winding thin, green florist's wire or picture-hanging wire around them. The wire doesn't really show but it holds the flowers firmly and gently in place. For dressy occasions, headbands can be covered with ribbon first or thin ribbon can be wrapped over the wire.

Roses were wired to this barrette and the stems hidden with ribbon.

You can make most floral decorations a day ahead. Leave the stems long enough to keep in water and put them in a refrigerator until you're ready to use them. For the occasion, simply cut the stems and put the band or barrette in your hair. I wear them to garden parties, summer dinners and even black-tie events. If you know what flowers you want to wear and have the materials close at hand, it should only take a few minutes to prepare your ornament. Long spiky flowers such as those of butterfly bush, delphinium and astilbe are easy to bend around a headband. Because leaves wilt first, it is usually better to strip the leaves off the flower before attaching it to the combs.

Straw hats are easily decorated with single flowers or clusters. The brim of the hat can be turned up and held with a decorated hatpin (perhaps the hatpin can hold a flower). Fresh flowers that wilt quickly can be placed in plastic floral tubes and arranged to cover the brim of the hat. Tuck the tubes into the hatband or attach with quick-dry glue or Velcro so you can take them out to fill with water and to change the flowers. The tubes will then have to be hidden by leaves, a ribbon or a hatband. Another florist's trick is to soak a tiny ball of cotton in water and poke it into the center of a trumpet-shaped flower. It won't be seen, but it will add moisture to help the flower stay fresh.

Flowers that last for a long time without being in water (see page 64) and flowers that dry naturally (see page 109) need only be pinned in place without too much fuss. Roses in bud, lavender, blue salvia, astilbe, celosia, delphinium and larkspur are especially useful. Have fun, be creative. Wrap the brim with trailing vines that hang down the back, place a nosegay on one side or group astilbes together to imitate feathers rising from the crown. The hat could even be used for a centerpiece, hung on a wall or worn to a wedding.

Flowers such as roses and honeysuckle make a fragrant and beautiful headband for a straw hat—perfect for a summer wedding.

Ideas for decorating hats with flowers are inspired by traditional hat designs. Real flowers are substituted for cloth, and spike-shaped flowers are used instead of feathers. Vines become the ribbons circling the brim.

A headband, a hatband or a choker can be made by sewing individual flowers onto a ribbon. If you would like it to last longer than a day or two the flowers can be dried in silica gel. You might, for example, sew hydrangea flower petals onto a ribbon, accenting the middle with a few rosebuds, cornflowers or other flowers that will dry naturally or last a few days without wilting. It is simple and quick to sew hydrangea petals on a ribbon a yard long. With a running stitch, small on the side with the flowers, large on the back side, each flower gets one stitch. It will take only about twenty minutes.

Individual hydrangea petals are sewn onto a ribbon to be used as a choker, hatband or headband.

Pin a rosebud to the neck of a blouse, on the lapel of a jacket, popping out of a pocket or tucked in a braid or ponytail. It will stay pretty all day and remind you of its presence with its fragrance.

Put a fragrant flower in your pocket and the perfume will stay with you all day. The entrance to our house is covered with honeysuckle, which is in full bloom in June and has sporadic blooms for the rest of the summer. Everyone who comes and goes through the front door is greeted by the most wonderful fragrance all summer long. When I go out, I frequently pick a blossom and put it in my pocket to carry a little of the garden with me.

FLOWERS OUT OF WATER

Even without water some flowers are slow to wilt. I picked assorted flowers on an overcast, hot and humid, 85-degree afternoon. When placed on my kitchen table, out of direct sunlight, they lasted long without looking wilted. It was, of course, no surprise that the everlastings (page 105), the flowers that air-dry, hold their color and shape indefinitely. It was a surprise to find that many other flowers easily hold their moisture for a day or two, even ones that will not air-dry. Here is a list of flowers that look good for a minimum of 24 hours. Experiment with your favorite flowers. You'll probably be surprised by the results.

Flowers laid on the table are a quick decoration for an impromptu dinner. Honeysuckle vines are laid on top of the trompe l'oeil honeysuckle painted on the table, and other flowers are scattered around.

A close-up of the above photo shows three clematis flowers and a
rose floating in a decorative bowl surrounded by the honeysuckle
and other flowers. Cornflowers, love-in-a-mist, rosebuds, blue salvias
and sedum 'Autumn Joy' (looking a little like broccoli) are spread
around the table and mixed with the honeysuckle.

24-HOUR FLOWERS AND FOLIAGE

Common Name	Latin Name
Blue salvia	*Salvia azurea*
Cockscomb	*Celosia*
Flowering maple (one, laid on its side, closed up gradually, while the one with its bell shape down and resting on the table looked perfect 48 hours later)	*Abutilon*
Hollyhock	*Alcea*
Hyacinth bean	*Dolichos lablab*
Ivy	*Hedera*
Japanese painted fern	*Athyrium Niponicum pictum*
Lamb's ear	*Stachys*
Larkspur 'Blue Elf'	*Delphinium*
Lavender	*Lavandula*
Lily (perfect for several days)	*Lilium*
Lungwort	*Pulmonaria*
Monkshood	*Aconitum*
Moss rose (closed after dark and opened in the morning light)	*Portulaca*
Pachysandra	*Pachysandra*
Passionflower	*Passiflora caerulea*
Plantain lily	*Hosta*
Rose	*Rosa*
Saint-John's-wort	*Hypericum*
Speedwell	*Veronica*
Spiraea	*Astilbe*
Strawflower	*Helichrysum bracteatum*
Vervain	*Verbena bonariensis*
Yarrow	*Achillea*

RECYCLE SPENT BOUQUETS

When discarding a bouquet of flowers I frequently sort out flowers for other uses. Flowers vary in how long they last in water. Some, such as Queen Anne's lace, may still look good after many flowers in the same arrangement have wilted. They can have their stems recut and be used in another bouquet. The colorful petals of other flowers can be collected for potpourri. Sometimes petals on roses are already dry and can be added straight to my potpourri jar. Others are laid on a well-ventilated basket or screen to finish drying. Keep them from direct sunlight and high humidity. After they have

Featured clockwise: a glass basket of potpourri with whole rosebuds; rose water tied with a white ribbon; rosemary-flavored olive oil; a fish memory jar; a bath sachet in a lace handkerchief; potpourri in a glass mustard jar and an egg cup; Christmas potpourri with pinecones, greens and cinnamon; a honey jar filled with ingredients for bath sachets; and a ceramic jar of rose paste.

dried, store them in an airtight jar. Flowers that air-dry, such as hydrangea, lavender and globe thistle, are hung in my drying closet to be used later in winter bouquets.

Approximately once a week rosebushes should have their spent blossoms removed. It is easy to gather soft rose petals, too, when I cut off spent blossoms. My trip to the rose garden serves two purposes: dead-heading (removing spent roses produces more roses) and gathering unblemished petals to dry or use fresh. Even though the flowers are wilted, the protected inside petals are perfect and their fragrance remains. They retain their color and fragrance longer if they are protected from direct sun and humidity. If gathered weekly, they can be saved over the summer for a multitude of little luxuries. Throw rose petals instead of rice at weddings; float rose petals in a bath to add fragrance and beauty "à la Cleopatra;" steep rose petals in boiling water to make rose water; use rose petals, the basic ingredient in potpourri, to scent your dresser drawers, closets or rooms; candy rose petals to decorate cakes or deserts (see recipes, pages 24–31.)

PRESSED FLOWERS AND FERNS UNDER GLASS

Glass-topped tables can be dressed up by pressing flowers, ferns or greens under the glass. Pressed flowers or ferns can be attached to glass tables by using a self-adhesive clear covering that preserves what it covers. If carefully stretched to avoid wrinkles, it is almost invisible. Add the pressed flowers to a picture frame or, better yet, put them inside the picture glass to surround the face of the portrait.

Pressed ferns are attached to the underside of a glass table with a clear self-adhesive covering. A miniature arrangement sits on the tabletop.

PRESSING FLOWERS

Pressed flowers are flowers that have been flattened and dried. They retain their color and take on a flat shape that makes them easy to use in decorating stationery, note cards, place cards and invitations. The more ambitious make pressed-flower pictures, which can be quite beautiful and very elaborate.

Pressing can be done in the old-fashioned schoolgirl way, putting the flowers between the pages of a heavy book. A wooden flower press, available from craft stores and garden catalogs, can be used with blotting paper, which more readily absorbs moisture and prevents mildew. It can take two to three weeks for the flowers to dry completely. I fill a press with flowers several times during the spring and summer and use them for the rest of the year. Pressed flowers, if kept dry and out of direct sunlight, will last for years. It is not always easy to identify a pressed flower, and I write in their identity with pencil on the blotting paper before I press them. Pressed flowers are even more fragile than dried flowers, and the smaller ones should be picked up only with tweezers and gently placed on top of a dot of glue or quick-drying cement.

When choosing flowers for pressing, try any you like. Here are some that reliably hold both their color and their shape:

FLOWERS FOR PRESSING

Common Name	Latin Name
Bleeding heart	*Dicentra spectabilis*
Checkered lily	*Fritillaria Meleagris*
Geranium	*Geranium*
Globeflower	*Trollius*

Common Name	Latin Name
Hydrangea blossoms, whole or the individual petals	*Hydrangea*
Larkspur	*Delphinium*
Lavender	*Lavandula*
Lungwort	*Pulmonaria*
Pansy	*Viola* × *Wittrockiana*
Primrose	*Primula*
Rose	*Rosa*
Sage	*Salvia*
Snowdrop	*Galanthus*
Violet	*Viola*
Wormwood	*Artemisia*

Try drying an assortment of foliage also. Three types that work well are delicately cut foliage as in ferns, parsley and bleeding hearts; silver-colored foliage as in artemisia, lamb's ears and dusty miller; and various small-leaved varieties of herbs such as thyme, sage and parsley.

THE GLAMOUR OF ROSE PETALS

Even to those unfamiliar with the language of flowers it is clear that roses mean love and beauty. As I am a hopeless romantic, I grow many. Rose petals, in days when home remedies prevailed, were believed to cheer the heart. Decorating with rose petals surely does. It dates back to the days of the Roman Empire, when roses and their petals adorned houses, dinner tables, drinking cups and food. Pillows were stuffed with rose petals, and wreaths and crowns were

Rose petals from two or three roses are enough to decorate a table for two.

made of them and worn as symbols of success. The guests at Nero's banquets had rose petals showered on them as they reclined until the floors were thick with blooms. The Romans couldn't grow enough to keep up with the demand, so they built greenhouses to grow roses in the winter and imported them by the shipload from North Africa. Roses are probably the most loved flowers on earth. They are one of the oldest recorded garden gifts.

ROSE CONFETTI TEA

Even after falling off the stem, rose petals hold their color and fragrance. They have many uses. I decorated a small table for a tea to celebrate an anniversary by scattering the cloth with rose petals, but any occasion and any table setting could be enhanced this way. Even when dropped at the base of a bouquet of roses the petals add interest and beauty.

Afternoon tea is a luxury for most Americans, a very pleasant celebration of an afternoon. For this occasion I have used a riot of petals from 'Betty Prior' roses, with single, open, six-petaled flowers. One bush of 'Betty Prior' roses is very prolific, blooming longer than most other roses, and easily provides petals for a romantic tea party. All of the petals in the photograph opposite came from one rose bush. The heart-shaped strawberry butter is made by blending several strawberries with a stick of sweet butter and chilling in a mold. The single rosebud on the napkin says, in the language of flowers (see page 163), "I love you." It will dry naturally and can be kept as a reminder of a wonderful afternoon. Violets are glued with a drop of egg white and readily stick on the sugar cubes, later to float in the tea.

POTPOURRI

Most of the long-lasting scent of potpourri comes not from the flower petals themselves but from drops of essential oils purchased from gift and craft shops. The essential oils have been perfected by experts and cover a wide range of fragrances and prices. Buy the essential oil of the fragrance you like best and add it to your favorite petals or whole dried flowers. Any petals can be scented to smell like rose, lavender or jasmine by putting a few drops of oil on the mixture, stirring gently, sealing in a jar or plastic bag and storing away from direct sunlight until ready to use.

My potpourri consists mostly of rose petals gathered throughout the summer and decorated with rosebuds picked when frost is expected in the fall. For contrasting color I add blue lavender, blue salvia, yellow sunflower petals and yellow calendula. Experiment to see what you like. You can't go wrong if you buy a scent that pleases you.

Look for unusual containers to hold potpourri: egg cups, brandy snifters, saltcellars. Glass mustard holders are a favorite because they have a lid with a hole that lets the fragrance escape but keeps dust out of the potpourri. For more fragrance, remove the top for a short time and then replace it. Keeping the mixture covered extends the life of the potpourri. Refresh the potpourri with some additional essential oils as needed.

MEMORY JAR—A GARDEN OF MEMORIES

Gardens hold many memories. My earliest memories involve lilies of the valley during my first year of school. My family lived two blocks from my grandparents, and my grandfather would pick me up and drive me the few blocks to school so I could give my teacher an armful of lilies of the valley gathered from his backyard. The fragrance lingers in my memory still. I have grown them every place I have lived since, but never have I been able to gather a bunch as large as the ones I remember my grandfather bringing from his small backyard. Occasionally I have sent a bouquet to cheer and scent the classroom for my children's teachers.

Visiting Ryan Gainey's garden shop, The Potted Plant, in Atlanta last year I found a memory jar, which is a large glass jar filled with dried flower heads or petals. The difference between potpourri and a memory jar is that each flower dropped in the jar carries with it the memory of a friend, a garden, a celebration or a love. It takes us back into the past and helps us remember special moments. Give a memory jar to a friend with a symbolic flower from your garden, perhaps a sweet sultan (*Centaurea moschata*) wishing happiness. Over time a garden itself becomes full of memories: for me, memories of friends who brought me plants, memories of the visit to a distant city where I purchased an unfamiliar plant, even memories of the first time I "met" the plants themselves.

NOSEGAY

Popular at the turn of the century, a nosegay is a small flower bouquet tied with lace and streamers of ribbon and meant to be carried, much like a bridesmaid's bouquet. The warmth of the hand releases the fragrance of the flowers. Today nosegays make a nice hostess present. Nosegays can even be used to decorate packages, or they can be placed at each guest's plate as a favor to take home, a remembrance of an enjoyable evening. The nosegay could be made with flowers that air-dry to last a season or conditioned fresh flowers bunched and tied with ribbons, doilies, raffia or lace. The nosegay can be kept with the bottoms of the stems in a short water glass in the refrigerator until ready to use. If properly conditioned (see page 174) they will last for half a day or longer out of water.

A fragrant nosegay of stocks, roses, ivy and lavender.

Floral foam attached to a plastic handle is frequently used for bridal bouquets and is another way to extend the life of a bouquet. This can be purchased from florists or flower-supply houses and is easy to decorate following the instructions for working with floral foam on page 179.

Give an everlasting nosegay. A small nosegay made of everlasting flowers can stay for weeks or months and dry naturally out of water, if it is not too humid (see list on page 109).

Globe thistle, cockscomb, craspedia 'Goldstick' and blue salvia make up this everlasting nosegay.

TOPIARY OF FRESH FLOWERS

Topiaries can be made of fresh or dried flowers. I place a short sturdy branch in a pot of ivy, balance a square block of floral foam on top and trim the corners with a sharp knife to create a rounded shape (It needn't be perfectly round. As you add flowers, their fullness will help shape the topiary.). After the floral foam is shaped, remove it from the branch and soak it for half an hour in warm water before replacing it on the branch and taping it in place. The topiary on page 79 uses Saint-John's-wort (*Hypericum*), lacecap hydrangea (*Hydrangea macrophylla*), balloon flower (*Platycodon grandiflorus*) and pincushion flower (*Scabiosa caucasica*). After the flowers wilt, save the floral foam and the branch to reuse.

Right: This fresh-flower topiary is arranged on top of a branch in a floral-foam ball and poked into a pot of ivy. The flowers are Saint-John's-wort, balloon flower, lacecap hydrangea and pincushion flower.

THE FOURTH OF JULY

One of the traditions in our family is a picnic on the beach to watch the fireworks. It becomes an event—a party with panache. Everything, of course, has to be in the red, white and blue theme, from the candy treats for the kids to the dessert for the adults and, of course, the flower arrangement. Start several days ahead, plan and do a little each day, so that when the holiday arrives you'll still be in a party mood. It's the last-minute hassles (everything takes longer than you thought and nothing can be found) that give headaches and make entertaining a nightmare.

Everything becomes more fun if there is something for all the senses: flowers for the eyes; food for the taste, and bright, knock-'em-out attention-getting colors and an element of surprise and humor (a rubber frog to make the children squeal or barefoot salt and pepper shakers from the flea market). It might seem like too much
trouble to take flowers on a picnic, but they add greatly to the sense of occasion. An arrangement in a basket, especially one with a handle, is easy to transport. If floral foam is used, there won't be any worry about water spilling. This year I found a garland of stars and several miniature flags in the local five and dime. These added to the surprise—who else would be crazy enough to carry flowers to a picnic? I made the arrangement the day before. I gathered red, white and blue flowers, looking for shapes that would give a feeling of a firecracker or an explosion. If you use your imagination, you might be able to see the spiral-shaped astilbes as rockets taking off; the drooping fuchsias, centers dangling, as bombs bursting; and the verbenas and achillea as the finale of the fireworks. Silly? Maybe, but it gets everyone in the mood of the party. I kept the basket of flowers in my cool basement until late afternoon and it was fine.

Remember to pack your sense of humor along with a rubber frog, whimsical salt and pepper shakers and a flower arrangement exploding with blooms for a Fourth of July picnic on the beach.

A red-and-blue tart made with blueberries and raspberries from the garden.

For Memorial Day or the Fourth of July an American flag can be made of flowers (blue verbena, red gaillardia and white gooseneck loosestrife) arranged in a flat basket of floral foam surrounded by moss.

GIFT WRAPPING

A small bouquet of flowers can make an unusual decoration for the top of a present. The flowers, if conditioned (see page 174), can be tied with a ribbon and placed on top of the package at the eleventh hour and will last many hours out of water, or they can be arranged in a floral-foam bouquet holder used for bridal bouquets (available from a florist's shop or floral-supply house).

Gifts can be decorated with flowers or greens year 'round. In the fall and winter, dried-flower arrangements make a practical and beautiful topping for a present (see page 105).

Left: Decorate a present with fresh flowers. Purple grape hyacinths, tulips, ranunculus *and virginia bluebells are arranged in a plastic floral foam bouquet holder.*

CHAPTER THREE

Autumn

*Flowers dress up everything—even a bowl of fruit. Water tubes hold-
ing nasturtiums, marigolds, cosmos 'Bright Lights' and coneflower
(Ratibida columnifera) can be poked between the pieces of fruit for
a colorful centerpiece.*

*The invariable mark of wisdom is to see the
miraculous in the common.*
—*Ralph Waldo Emerson*

The garden's gifts are available year 'round, but the abundance of the harvest comes at summer's end in early fall. This is a wonderful time to introduce a friend to the wonders of the garden; perhaps he or she will become a gardener too. Take a basket filled with the garden's harvest to a neighbor.

Give a basket of different kinds of tomatoes, so many of which are available only from the garden, such as 'Pink Girl Hybrid', 'Yellow Pear' or 'Lemon Boy', to introduce your friends to unique flavors. If you grow onions, garlic or carrots, braid their long stems together and then give them to a friend. On occasion I have even braided several flower stems together before hanging them to dry. After they dry, they only need the addition of a ribbon or perhaps a bundle of dried grasses to become a decorative swag.

Vegetables are beautiful and colorful. Make a centerpiece for the kitchen table out of the vegetables harvested before the first frost and the whole family is reminded of the earth's fruitfulness. There's an added advantage: Fewer of them will spoil—as they sometimes do when packed away, out of sight, in a cupboard.

Summer into early fall is also the time to plan ahead for winter's scarcity. Harvest everlastings (see list, page 109) and dry them

Vegetables are beautiful and colorful, and they make a wonderful centerpiece for the kitchen table. Pictured here are sunflowers, assorted tomatoes, 'Jack-Be-Little' pumpkins, green peppers, eggplants, marigolds, cosmos, zinnias and purple ruffled basil.

A variety of seashore grasses and small branches with brightly colored fall leaves make a colorful arrangement in an umbrella stand. Other possibilities include various hydrangea and the fluffy seedpods of clematis vines.

for winter bouquets, gifts and Christmas decorations. In autumn, when the trees undress, gather some leaves to brighten the indoors. Fall leaves, with all the beauty of their bright sunset colors, will last long enough to brighten a mantel for Thanksgiving if gently ironed on low heat between two pieces of waxed paper. The wax lightly coats the leaves, keeping them from crinkling up, and adds a dull shine that enhances their color.

Corkscrew euonymus branches will last in water for many weeks, the leaves holding their bright red color. The branches, even without the leaves, are sculptural, twisted like corkscrews. Subtly veined with light green, the branches are beautiful.

A variety of small branches from different trees can be picked and arranged indoors in water, where they can be enjoyed for several weeks. For large arrangements, I use an umbrella stand and mix in tall, roadside grasses.

MAIL FLOWERS FROM YOUR GARDEN

Spring and fall are good times to send garden flowers through the mail to friends in other areas. The weather in most parts of the country is cool so they won't wilt from high heat in transit, and post offices and mail services guarantee overnight delivery. Many of the flowers we buy in florists' shops have traveled long distances out of water from their growing fields in South America, Holland and even Australia. One of the longest-lasting shipped flowers is the peony, traditionally picked by commercial growers when the bud is fat and starting to show some color. Peonies have a great capacity for holding water and will keep in cold storage for three weeks laid flat in vented boxes. When placed in water they will revive, look good in bud and open in a week. When they are displayed in wholesale flower markets they are lying on counters bunched together, out of water. The trick is to pick flowers in bud and condition them well (see page 174) before you send them on their way. If on arrival they are wilted and dehydrated, they can be easily resuscitated by recutting the stems on a slant and dipping them in boiling water for thirty seconds before placing them in a deep bucket of warm water to condition them again before arranging.

J. Barry Ferguson, a notable floral designer recommends that the box in which flowers are to be shipped be lined with bubble wrap or foam, to help insulate from heat and cold. Soft tissue paper can be crinkled under the neck of the flowers to hold the heads in place and keep the necks from breaking. The bottom of the stems can be wrapped with damp newspaper and placed in a plastic bag to keep them moist and cool. A plastic bag should not be sealed over the flower heads as it could encourage high humidity and heat, which together make the flowers mature and open sooner.

Right: Peonies are one of the longest-lasting flowers while in bud, which makes them perfect for shipping through the mail out of water. J. Barry Ferguson arranged peonies and clarkias with dried starflower, Queen Anne's lace picked from a roadside and silver-leaved eucalyptus purchased from a florist.

TOO MUCH ZUCCHINI

Six zucchini plants planted in spring will more than feed my family of seven, weekend guests and neighbors all summer. After boiling, sautéing and baking tiny zucchini, and puréeing larger ones for bread and soup, we still are surprised to find several hiding, in spite of their baseball-bat size, under even larger leaves. Conventional wisdom in peaceful Vermont advises locking cars at shopping centers to avoid finding your backseat filled with a generous donation of zucchini left by a kind, overproductive gardener.

One playful solution is to turn the largest zucchini into a peacock centerpiece. You will need:

1 baseball-bat–size zucchini
Assorted long-stemmed flowers
Ferns
2 bell peppers
Floral foam
Floral tape
Knife
Spoon
Small-leaved ivy
Cockscomb celosia
Queen Anne's lace

If you don't have the flowers I used, substitute your own or florist's flowers for an original variation.

Place the zucchini on an oval platter and position it so that the neck points upward. Slice just enough off the bottom, ¼ inch or so, to allow it to sit flat. Next scoop out an oval near the back of the zucchini for your peacock's tail. Remove all the seeds (the

zucchini you scoop out can be used for making bread or soup).
Now cut a section of floral foam to fill the hole. Soak the shaped
floral foam in warm water for a half hour. When placed in the
opening, the floral foam will add weight and help balance the flower
arrangement. While the floral foam is soaking, pick your flowers.
The best flowers have arching shapes; they will form a graceful tail
that can be viewed from all sides. If it is to be viewed from three
sides, arrange the flowers straight in a fan shape, like the fan of a
strutting peacock. Look for round, brightly colored flowers to fashion the "eyes" of the circle design found in the tail of a real peacock.

Fill the hole in the zucchini with the soaked floral foam. The
head, beak and comb are fashioned from lightweight, colorful peppers and attached with straight pins. Slice an opening for the beak.
As the pepper dries over the next few hours, the beak will open.
A flower can even be inserted in the mouth. Use a layer of ferns to
shape the wings and tail feathers. Small-leaved ivy forms a collar
where the neck and body meet and where the head meets the neck.
The crushed velvet of cockscomb provides the peacock's comb. You
can add a frilled collar of Queen Anne's lace around the neck. The
peacock may be a little quirky, but it amuses guests and the seeds
of a smile are planted.

"He who makes a garden
Works hand in hand with God."
—*Douglas Malloch*

Different vegetables will inspire other fun projects. Having an abundance of radishes, I decorated a plain water glass with a bunch. First I placed two large rubber bands around the glass, one near the top and one near the bottom. The radishes are easily tucked under the rubber bands and placed around the glass. The rubber bands were hidden with raffia. I filled the glass with roadside flowers and used it as a centerpiece. For a more elegant, uptown version, asparagus can also be used the same way.

Radishes arranged around a water glass, held with a rubber band hidden by ivy, is an interesting vase for roadside flowers: black-eyed Susans, Queen Anne's lace, gaillardias and garden-grown zinnias.

Melons, gourds, cabbages and even peppers make unusual candle holders or vases. Cabbages with their many pockets work especially well, as the spaces between the leaves hold small amounts of water and flowers can be tucked into them easily. After the flowers in the arrangement fade, the cabbage can still be cooked and eaten.

Green and red peppers are used as vases to hold Queen Anne's lace, scarlet runner bean flowers and black-eyed Susans.

Because a cabbage can hold water between its leaves, it can be used to hold roses or other flowers.

PRESERVING A LITTLE OF
THE GARDEN FOR WINTER

Vinegars can be flavored with herbs for a winter treat. It is good to let them steep for a month or longer to flavor the vinegar before using. Decorative bottles are readily available from hardware stores and gift catalogs. I use white wine vinegar as a base and flavor each bottle with the bouquet of one herb. Basil, thyme, dill, tarragon and chives are my favorite flavors, but any herb will do. If you use purple basil, the vinegar will turn a cheery red, which makes a nice

White wine vinegars flavored with herbs steep on the windowsill.
Dill, chives, purple basil and green basil are pictured here.

Christmas present. Vinegars can also be flavored with berries to make interesting salad dressings; try raspberries or blueberries, my favorites.

Olive oils are flavored in the same way. Simply tuck several sprigs of your favorite herb in the bottle. All of the flavored oils work for salad dressings but many are also good for marinating meat and vegetables. Rosemary oil when mixed with a little Dijon mustard is good for marinating lamb, and basil oil is a perfect base for sauces with tomatoes.

Fragrant Herb Bundles

Prepare and give a freshly picked herb bundle, a bouquet garni, to a friend who likes to cook. Bouquets garnis are traditionally simmered in a stockpot or laid under a roast, flavoring the meat as well as the gravy, but they can also be decorative, hung on a kitchen pot rack. A traditional bouquet garni combines fresh celery leaves, parsley, thyme and bay leaves in a small bundle.

Give a dried one to a friend who loves to barbecue and another one for a friend's fireplace, where it will release its fragrance in winter. Fresh or dried herb bundles can decorate a present, too. Bundle herbs together for air drying, using the same method as for drying flowers (see page 105).

Herb Sachets for the Bath

From medieval times, herbs have added fragrance to the bath and helped relieve bodily aches and pains. Tie a sachet under the faucet, and as the bath fills, the rushing hot water will release the perfume of the oils and condition the water, creating another of life's little luxuries.

BATH SACHET

1 cup oatmeal (not instant)
½ cup rosemary leaves (or substitute lavender,
thyme, lemon verbena, comfrey or your favorite
herb)
¼ cup rose petals (optional)

Mix the ingredients together and, for each sachet, place a few tablespoons in the center of a six-inch square of lace, cheesecloth or muslin. Bring the four corners together and tie in the middle with a washable ribbon, making sure that the mixture is secure in your bag. Tie the bag to hang directly under the faucet before you start your bath. Makes 8 sachets.

I keep additional sachet mixture in a honey pot in the bathroom and refill my sachet as necessary. Each bag can be used several times before it needs refilling. Oatmeal is very good for the skin but by itself is not particularly attractive, which is why I add rose petals. The rose petals complement the oatmeal and add a little more fragrance to the mix.

For a humorous present for friends with a hot tub, sew a large tea bag from cheesecloth or muslin, fill it with a mixture of herbs and oatmeal (keeping the same proportions as in the recipe) and staple the bag to a string. Write the message "tea for two" on a piece of paper and attach it to the other end of the string. The "tea" bag can be used several times.

Herb Wreath

At summer's end, make a fresh herb wreath in floral foam and let it dry naturally while hanging on the kitchen wall. Remember, as the herbs dry they shrink, so pack the wreath full and, if needed, add more herbs later. The herbs can be used from the wreath or it can be purely decorative. The decorative wreath in the photograph below features an assortment of culinary and decorative herbs: oregano, thyme, rosemary, lavender, parsley, sage, garlic chives, tansy, artemisia and lamb's ears.

A fresh herb wreath.

Dried Herbs

Dried herbs can be chopped and stored in bottles or zip-lock bags for use over the winter. They are more flavorful than purchased, packaged herbs. When put in decorative bottles, they are welcome presents for cooks. Hang herbs for drying using the same method as for drying flowers (see page 105).

A dried mixed herb bouquet can be used whole or chopped and stored in plastic bags as prepared at Mohonk Mountain House.

ORNAMENTAL BERRIES FOR FALL ARRANGEMENTS

Notice the various decorative berries growing wild along the road-side. Bittersweet is usually the most conspicuous with its bright orange and yellow berries, perfect for creating long-lasting fall arrangements. Invite some of the lesser-known ornamental berries into your yard such as beauty-berry and porcelain vine. Beauty-berry is covered with the brightest purple berries all fall. The branches can be picked and sprayed with lacquer so they'll last longer indoors.

A grapevine wreath when decorated with dried flowers will last several seasons.

Porcelain vine is available with plain or variegated leaves and will grow in partially shaded areas. Looking out at the garden from an upstairs window, you'll notice the variegated leaves appear to be dusted with snow all summer and sparkle in the sunlight. But the vine looks best when covered with berries in the fall, each a subtly mottled shade of blue, purple, pink or cream as delicate as porcelain. With such natural beauty, a simple arrangement will suffice and the berries spill naturally from the blue wineglass shown in the photograph here. I remove a few of the leaves along the ends of the sprays to expose more berries.

Mottled shades of blue, purple, pink and cream porcelain berries spilling out of a wineglass.

*Rose hips are the fruit of the rosebush and are decorative in
arrangements.*

Some rosebushes hold their hips (fruits) throughout the winter
and can be picked as needed and used fresh in arrangements. The
smaller rose hips, those the size of pearls, can be picked in early
fall and sprayed with clear lacquer. They will last for a year or two
and can be used in dried-flower arrangements, mixed with greens
at Christmas for wreaths, centerpieces and candle cups.

The fall arrangement by designer J. Barry Ferguson in the photograph below celebrates the season with bursting branches of various ornamental berries and rose hips falling out of a Chinese wooden bucket. Even a thin branch from an old apple tree holds the last apples of fall. Inside the bucket, Barry has stuffed apples and the unusual green knobby Osage oranges. The Osage orange is an ornamental fruit from the American native bowwood tree, or *Maclura*, a deciduous tree once widely used in the Midwest for field hedges and even earlier by Native Americans for making bows.

This autumn arrangement of berries, rose hips, apples and Osage oranges was designed by J. Barry Ferguson to last for many weeks when arranged in moist floral foam.

The variety and availability of interesting berries is endless. Some of the smaller varieties can be sprayed with hair spray or lacquer to hold their shape and color longer. Plan to pick a few of these for fall arrangements.

Beauty-berry: Bright purple or white berries are conspicuously displayed as the leaves turn yellow and drop off the bushes in early autumn.

Viburnum: Different varieties are available bearing black, red, yellow, orange and blue berries, but the red varieties are the most conspicuous. They all have creamy white, flat clusters of flowers in summer.

Roses: Red or orange rose hips come in various sizes, depending on the variety of rosebush.

Pyracantha: Red, reddish orange or yellow conspicuous berries on spiny shrubs are frequently espaliered on a wall or the side of a house.

Porcelain berry: Mottled berries the size of peas in shades of blue, rose and purple grow on long graceful arching branches, vigorously climbing up trees or on the sides of buildings.

Bittersweet: Yellow berries that dry as they open, revealing an orange-red center. This is a twisting, twining vine that loves to climb trees and shrubs and needs watching and pruning in a garden to keep it from hurting its neighbors. However, the little extra care needed is repaid by its fall beauty.

EVERLASTING FLOWERS

Winter, with all the holidays it brings, can be made brighter with the colorful flowers of everlastings. Everlastings are flowers that dry naturally and are preserved in their true flower shape and color. Some everlastings, strawflower and statice, for example, have papery petals that look the same whether fresh or dry. The reds of celosia, the blues of salvia and the many colors of statice and strawflowers will stay bright throughout winter and beyond when dried. Some, such as roses and lavender, hold their fragrance for many months.

The best way to save everlasting flowers for fall and winter bouquets is to cut them just before the fall peak of bloom. The longer you leave them out after they bloom, the more likely rain or wind will damage their perfection. Flowers for drying should be cut in the heat of the day. Rather than conserving moisture, as with cut flowers, with everlastings you squander it. Strip off the leaves and hang the flowers upside down in small bunches held together by rubber bands around the stems in a dark, warm, dry place. As they dry and shrink, the rubber band will continue to hold the flowers, and the weight of the flowers will pull the stems straight while they dry and stiffen. Once dried, they'll last until fresh-flower time next spring. Because we are close to the sea and have very humid summers, we have a small closet with a dehumidifier where we dry flowers. Without it, the flowers mildew and rot rather than dry.

ODE TO HYDRANGEAS

Hydrangeas! We need an "ode to hydrangeas," one of Mother Nature's greatest gifts: the peegee hydrangeas with their cone-shaped soft, cotton-candy fluffs in a blushing pink, lacecap hydrangeas delicate as their name, and the big-leaf or mop-headed hydrangeas in their blue or pink shades. I manage to squeeze some of each into my garden. Coming into bloom in July, the fleecy, overblown blossoms hang on the bushes for six months or longer and change color subtly as the cool weather comes, refusing to be deterred by stormy weather. They cling and they cling, and I pick and I pick. Only a few at first, when the petals feel leathery to the touch, because I wouldn't rob the shrub or be without flowers in the garden. The ones I pick I hang in a drying closet for the unblemished blossoms in my Christmas arrangements. As fall approaches, I pick a large arrangement and put it in water to dry slowly as the water evaporates. By putting them in water, I can add branches of colored leaves or flowers that need water to stay fresh and bright. Corkscrew euonymus branches with their green veins and scarlet-red leaves combine well with the leaves and berries of viburnums, and both complement hydrangea blossoms in shape and color. After the euonymus and the viburnums droop and brown, the hydrangeas are still going strong, the last to leave the party. I reuse them in other dried arrangements.

An arrangement of hydrangeas, the red berries of viburnums and branches of corkscrew euonymus brings the vibrant colors of fall indoors.

Even in November, a few remain to be picked. These have some blemishes, but they also have a strong purple-blue color or are a deeper rose, and I can hide the blemishes by turning the best side out as I arrange them. Because hydrangeas bloom on new branches each year, I am really pruning as I go along and I have less to clean up in the fall. Hydrangeas have become, over the years, the staples of my Christmas decorating and dried-flower arrangements.

Joan Williams makes good use of an unfinished closet by hanging
flowers to dry before arranging them into winter bouquets. The
flowers in the bottles have been dried in silica gel and attached to
wire stems.

FLOWERS FOR AIR DRYING INCLUDE:

Ageratum	Joe-pye weed
Artemisia	Lavender
Astilbe	Plumed thistle
Baby's breath	Safflower
Bells-of-Ireland	Sea lavender
Blue salvia	Sedum 'Autumn Joy'
Calendula	Statice
Celosia	Strawflower
Dusty miller	Veronica
Echinops	Winged everlasting
Golden rod	Xeranthemum
Hydrangea	Yarrow
Iron weed	

Some flowers have sculptural seedpods that dry naturally and hold their shape and color through the winter. These I collect from the garden and wild from fields and roadsides. They can make a simple yet elegant fall decoration when placed in a bowl on a table or a box next to a fireplace. Look around your area and you'll find many more. Flowers with sculptural seedpods include:

Black-eyed Susan	Mexican hat
Chinese lantern	Milkweed
Clematis	Pinecone
Columbine	Poppy
Coneflower	Staghorn sumac
Gaillardia	Starflower
Honesty	Thistle
Love-in-a-mist	

A variety of seedpods, pinecones and dried flowers can be used to decorate a basket. The pinecones can be wired onto the basket, while the smaller seedpods and dried flowers can be glued (Elmer's glue or a quick-drying cement works well).

Also, remember the many ornamental grasses and their plumes that air-dry can embellish a dried-flower arrangement. For an unexpected and colorful addition, air-dry ornamental peppers.

Dried flowers and seedpods are fragile and should be handled carefully. If they are to be used in dried bouquets and the stems are weak or break off while drying, green floral wire or floral picks with wire attached can be wound around the stem for strength or can replace the stem entirely.

Dry floral foam or Styrofoam can be used as a base for arranging bouquets of dried flowers. Styrofoam comes in a variety of shapes and can be used for making any number of dried-flower arrangements from Christmas trees to topiaries. Use a pencil or other pointed object to make a hole in the Styrofoam. Squeeze a drop of quick-drying cement into the hole and push the flower gently into place. After your arrangement is complete, spray with an unscented hair spray to hold your fragile flower petals in place. To dust a longer-lived arrangement, use a hair dryer on a low setting to blow off the dust gently.

Right: A basket is decorated with pinecones, Nigella *seedpods, wheat, starflowers, strawflowers and the spiny fruit of the sweet gum tree.*

Dried cockscombs, starflowers, larkspurs and astilbes are arranged
in glass vases filled with potpourri.

WATER-DRYING FLOWERS

Water drying is a slower process than hanging the flowers to dry. The advantage is you can enjoy the flowers fresh for a week or two and then hang them for later use in dried arrangements. When it is time to throw a wilted flower arrangement on the compost heap, look more closely. Some of the flowers—rosebuds, lavender, baby's breath—will have already started drying. If they are not completely dry, add them to your drying room collection or leave them in water. The stems might not dry straight, but they may be more interesting if gracefully curved; if straight stems are a must, they can be wired to artificial stems.

As you read through this book you will see many uses for dried flowers: decorating baskets, decorating packages and picture frames, as well as making nosegays, winter bouquets, and Christmas decorations. Dried-flower arrangements can be even more colorful when displayed in glass vases filled with potpourri or rose petals.

THANKSGIVING

Instead of bouquets of flowers at Thanksgiving, evoke the spirit of the occasion by celebrating the harvest with piles of fruit and vegetables. A mantel, a wreath or a centerpiece can be beautifully seasonal when decorated with baby vegetables, ornamental corn, 'Jack-Be-Little' pumpkins, fall leaves, vines of Boston ivy, leaves and berries of viburnum, lady apples and tiny pears. Festive, cheery and unusual, they combine all the traditional symbols of Thanksgiving to bring the spirit of the first Thanksgiving into your home.

Dishes shaped like vegetables are a very popular motif, but it can be more fun to use vegetables themselves as dishes. When

Boston ivy is draped on a mantel with fall leaves and miniature pumpkins, eggplant, apples, pears and Indian corn.

Fall leaves, dried flowers and berries and miniature pumpkins, corn and gourds surround a hollowed-out pumpkin used as a soup tureen.

hollowed out, many vegetables can be used as vases for flowers (eggplant, acorn squash, peppers) or even as serving bowls (for soup, as in the case of pumpkins and other round squash). A large pumpkin with the top and seeds removed will make an interesting soup tureen. At Halloween I've filled one with chili for a children's party and at Thanksgiving with a squash soup for the grown-ups. The base of the pumpkin tureen is the same reusable grapevine wreath from spring (see page 13) interwoven with bittersweet and decorated with strawflowers and Chinese lanterns. The fall leaves are the dark-burgundy Boston ivy, the yellow fringed leaves of Japanese maple and royal-purple oak leaves.

CHAPTER FOUR

Winter

A Victorian mantel draped with garlands and decorated with dried hydrangeas, gold ribbons and strings of "pearls."

Apparently with no surprise
To any happy flower,
The frost beheads it at its play
In accidental power.

The blond assassin passes on,
The sun proceeds unmoved
To measure off another day
For an approving God.
                              Emily Dickinson

In most of the country, winter brings the bleakest weather with short days and low temperatures, but it also brings the festive month of December. For me, Christmas is the brightest spot of winter, when the flame of giving burns high—a time of optimism, hope and good cheer. It is a time of generosity and of gathering together with family and friends. All my children come home, if only for a night. December is the busiest month of the year for mothers and the slowest for children. Christmas is a favorite holiday, with decorated trees twinkling, hidden packages and the children's impatient, "When will Christmas be here?" The splendor of the season, with its mixture of wonder and awe, excitement and anticipation, generosity and love, manifests itself in the boughs of garden greens and Christmas trees that bring fragrance, warmth and beauty into the house. It makes it easier to accept being chased indoors by the blustering, snow-laden winds.

I start dressing the house in greens the first week in December, extending the joyous season by leisurely decorating a little at a time. A house decorated with greens, dried flowers, pinecones, seedpods and berries reminds everyone who enters of Nature's infinitely versatile bounty and her timeless beauty. No gilding is necessary, and I wouldn't consider spray painting anything from the garden. The garden's gifts, with their simple dignity, easily can hold their own and coexist compatibly with golden ribbons, pearls and other man-made decorations.

The possibilities for Christmas decorations from the garden are endless. Many of the ideas that follow can be changed or mixed for interesting variations. As you decorate from year to year you will be building on what you learned the year before. Even though Christmas boasts such a wealth of tradition, nothing stays exactly the same in my house and each year shows improvements.

Inspiration from times past can enrich the present. On page 116, a Victorian-inspired fireplace combines the opulence of fake pearls, gilded mirrors and golden ribbons with the garden's naturally dried beauties: hydrangea, blue salvia, celosia, gomphrena and baby's breath. What you do this year in your home could be the start of your own traditions, ones your children could borrow and continue in their own way.

WREATHS

Until recent years I thought winter was not a time for gardens and certainly not a time to pick arrangements for the house. Previously, my own winter garden began with pine tree branches, picked for indoor use at Christmas, and ended with forcing forsythia branches occasionally after January first. Several years ago in mid-February, Peter Stevens, a friend and professional floral designer, amazed me with the variety of textures and colors on a wreath he had made from plants picked from a winter woodland garden under snow. In the wreath Peter designed, he combined variegated *Euonymus* leaves with the narrow, deep-burgundy leaves of *Leucothoe*, silver-gray lavender sprigs, the marbled, broad leaves of hardy *Cyclamen* and perky, red rose hips. The wreath is made on a floral foam ring and can be hung or used flat as a centerpiece.

This wreath is made exclusively with things picked from a northern garden in February. The wreath includes variegated euonymus, burgundy leucothoe, silver-gray lavender sprigs, marbled cyclamen leaves and red rose hips.

A wreath can be hung on a door or a wall or placed on a table, perhaps with a hurricane lamp in the center.

CHRISTMAS PRESENTS
FROM THE GARDEN

*Christmas-present ideas from the garden abound and anything
you like is sure to please a friend. Here are some suggestions
for things that can be made ahead for gifts at Christmas:*

Bath sachets
Braided vegetables
Dried-flower arrangements
Dried-flower wreaths
Dried-herb wreaths
Dried herbs or herb mixes
Dried nosegays
Herb oils

Herb- or fruit-flavored vinegars
Jars of roasted sunflower seeds
Miniature dried arrangements
Potpourri
*Pressed-flower picture frames or
    flower pictures*
Pressed-flower note cards or stationery
Christmas decorations from the garden

Georgia Wall designed this attractive
way to display a dried-flower wreath.
Jars of fresh cranberries amazingly
hold their bright color and last for a
year as a kitchen decoration. The jars
act as a stand for the dried-flower
wreath, which is made from vines
and covered with moss.

PINECONE WREATH

Every year I bring out my pinecone wreath. It is eight years old and was given to me by a good friend, Martha ("Puddy") Kraska. It is wonderful to be reminded of special friends with a gift that you can use year after year. Most years I have only hung a ribbon on it and used it without any changes. At the end of the holiday season I wrap it for protection and return it to the attic, to bring out again the following year.

Martha made the wreath by winding picture wire around pinecones to secure them to a wire frame that can be purchased at a nursery, Christmas shop or craft supply store. The pinecones were gathered and the tightly closed ones were spread on a cookie sheet to bake in a low oven (200 degrees Fahrenheit) for a few minutes to hurry the drying process and open the cones' scales. Watch them closely to prevent the tips of the scales from burning. This is a simple but messy process as the pinecones ooze a dark sap. Be sure to wear gloves and to cover your cookie sheet with aluminum foil. After they have cooled, some of the larger pinecones can be cut to a uniform size. Twist the thin wire around the individual pinecones, under their scales where it won't show, and wire each pinecone individually to the wire frame. The first pinecones added will wobble, but as more are added, they brace each other and the wreath becomes stable.

This year is my pinecone wreath's eighth birthday and it needed a little repair; the tips of some pinecones had chipped off. I wanted to hang a natural wreath, one that wouldn't be hurt by the weather, on the garden gate. Using a tube of cement glue, I added some fresh pinecones, seedpods, fern fronds and rose hips. Red rose hips, the fruits that form on the rosebush after the flowers drop, add Christmas cheer to your wreath. They will keep indefi-

An all-natural wreath of pinecones, dried seedpods and rose hips is hardy enough to hang outside all winter long.

nitely if sprayed with a clear lacquer. I tried to have as many different shades of brown as possible. I sprayed the whole wreath again with lacquer (a matte varnish to bring out the color and add a sheen but not a high gloss) and this year left the ribbon off. Next year perhaps I'll add a mixture of nuts—walnuts, pecans, and almonds, all in different shades of brown and varied in texture and shape. There are so many possibilities!

A miniature Christmas tree is built in a wreath and decorated with dollhouse miniatures.

CHRISTMAS-TREE WREATHS

December is the month to trim boxwood hedges and collect the clippings for Christmas decorations. Boxwood is fragrant and long-lasting indoors, looking fresh for many weeks. Florist shops frequently feature small trees made of boxwood on a floral-foam form. It is easy enough to do yourself. Cut the floral foam in the shape of a Christmas tree and soak it in warm water for half an hour. The boxwood easily pokes into the wet floral foam. Form a small Christmas tree by starting with larger pieces at the bottom and gradually ending with short pieces at the top. One stem should point straight up at the top to emphasize the tree shape. Decorate your Christmas tree with small ornaments, dried flowers, ribbons or whatever you choose. A small tree-shaped piece of floral foam can be wired onto a pine wreath, covered with boxwood on three sides and decorated with dollhouse miniatures to make an unusual wreath that guests will want to view up close.

Lilies are beautifully set off, blooming in an evergreen wreath. At this time of year, of course, they must be purchased from a florist, but a wreath needs only a few lilies, and several flowers bloom on one stem. Lilies will last in individual water tubes for at least a week. Buy them right before Christmas and they will last until New Year's. Many other fresh flowers will work as well: red gerbera daises, fragrant freesias and red tulips. Choose what you like and design your own wreath. A ribbon twisted around the wreath will dress it up.

Lilies in plastic tubes of water decorate an evergreen wreath.

GRAPEVINE WREATH

A grapevine wreath can be completely changed with the seasons to celebrate each in its turn, or it can be decorated (as is the one in the photograph) to last through many seasons or even year 'round. With the addition of different color ribbons and other appropriate material, special seasons can be emphasized; try, for instance, red or green ribbon for Christmas, perhaps with cinnamon sticks and pinecones.

The simplicity of an all-natural, earth-tone wreath covered with dried flowers, cones, acorns, nuts, burrs, seed capsules, bare twigs and seedpods has a timeless dignity and is appropriate the year 'round.

This grapevine wreath combines the fragile and delicate lacecap hydrangea with golden dried yarrow, love-in-a-mist and poppy seedpods, as well as the sculptural starflower pods, wisps of wheat and stands of purple statice.

MANTELPIECE DECORATIONS

For the decoration in the photograph on page 116, use a garland (princess pine) five times the length of the fireplace mantel to be covered (or attach several garlands to equal this length). The garlands are doubled and twisted back and forth across the whole length of the fireplace mantel. It is important to create a full and completely covered look. If your mantel is wide enough, the weight of the boughs will hold the garlands on the fireplace. I've used double-stick tape (for holding thirty-pound pictures), but be careful it doesn't remove the paint.

The sign "I Believe in Santa" is from the American Crafts Museum in New York City and is hung with wire as a picture would be. On top of the mirror, where it doesn't show, is my double-sided, all-purpose tape that holds the garlands surrounding the mirror.

The fleecy blue blossoms of hydrangea were gathered over the summer and throughout the fall when their brightly colored petals felt leathery. Other dried flowers mixed with green garlands will work just as nicely. Every year the decorations are different, reflecting what I grew the summer before. Celosia (red is especially festive), the jewel tones of globe amaranth (*Gomphrena*) and multicolored statice all work well.

Your mantel might not come together all at once. Arrange it, stand back and look at it. Study it and move the flowers around. Sometimes designs work immediately, but most often they need to be arranged, looked at, moved, looked at again, and often moved slightly one more time. Sometimes when I put up a mantel and walk by the next day, I see an area that needs more flowers, so I add a few.

A close-up of the Victorian mantel shown on page 116.

Christmas Mantels

Returning more and more to an old-fashioned, all-natural Christmas, a mantel can be quietly elegant when covered with juniper and its blue berries, the draping greens of golden-tipped cedar and dwarf, hard fruits such as lady's apples and seckel pears.

A miniature village of wooden buildings can be placed on rolls of cotton batting to give it a snowy appearance. Four- and six-inch twigs of pines and evergreens may be arranged to resemble miniature trees.

Heralding a return to an old-fashioned Christmas, a mantel is quietly elegant when covered with juniper and its blue berries, the draping greens of golden-tipped cedar and dwarf, and hard fruits such as lady's apples and seckel pears.

Oak moss has been glued to the exterior of an inexpensive plastic sleigh and three reindeer. The sleigh is filled with variegated and plain holly, and the reindeer are dressed with ribbons and attached to the sleigh with golden reins.

CHRISTMAS TREE DECORATIONS

A Miniature in Santolina

Use a Styrofoam tree shape or cut a brick of floral foam into a Christmas-tree shape, six inches wide at the bottom, tapering to a point eight inches tall. Turn the tree on its side and cut it in half lengthwise to create a two-inch-wide floral foam base. Starting at the bottom, gently push three-inch-long pieces of santolina into and around the base. Continue up the whole length of the tree with each layer slightly narrower than the layer before. At the top, place one two-inch sprig pointing straight up to define the shape of the tree. Use three thin, quarter-inch-wide ribbons, two yards long. Cut the ribbons in half. Tie three together into one bow in the middle of the length of ribbon. Place the bow on top of the tree. Repeat with the other three ribbons and place the second bow at right angles to the first on top of the tree. Fasten them with a small artificial bird, ornament or dried flowers. Gently twist and wrap the bow's streamers in soft S-shaped curves down the sides of the tree. Tuck in the ends. Next add dried flowers— rosebuds, pink and purple globe amaranths (*Gomphrena*), celosia and plumed thistle. Continue to turn the tree as you decorate to make all sides and views even. The tree can be placed directly on a table or raised on top of a silver baby cup or an upside-down flowerpot.

A miniature Christmas tree made from dried santolina.

An Ivy Christmas Tree

Ivy topiaries in different shapes are available from garden stores and floral shops. This ivy topiary, right, is four years old and it has been no trouble to maintain. Rarely pruned, it weaves its small leaves in and out of the frame with little help from me. Some of the more curving topiaries, especially the smaller animals, need more attention and are not as easy to keep.

Groups of red and white gomphrena balls dot the tree at Christmas. Their stems are strong enough to be poked directly into the ivy's wire frame. The base of the topiary is wrapped in Spanish moss to hide the soil. Ribbons again add a festive and finished touch. The topiary sits on an antique sled piled high with presents to greet family and friends on Christmas Eve.

A topiary ivy tree decorated with ribbons and red and white gomphrena flowers.

DRIED-FLOWER CHRISTMAS TREE

For a very special Christmas, a tree made entirely from dried flowers can be a spectacular focal point. It is not difficult to make, but it does take planning to grow the flowers necessary to cover the form. Grapevines twisted into a Christmas-tree form are available from craft and Christmas shops. Flowers are easily poked into the form and wedged between the vines. No tying or gluing is necessary unless you plan to move the tree. I first covered the tree on page 135 with hydrangea blossoms because they were plentiful and could serve as a base. Their stems alone, poked into the frame, held them in place. Three mature hydrangea shrubs will more than furnish the necessary blossoms. Artemisia is a good alternative to hydrangea. Lace was wrapped around and between the blossoms, hiding the frame. Battery-operated lights were added next, and the cords were carefully woven underneath the blossoms to the wire. Celosias, plumed thistles and pink globe amaranths (*Gomphrena*) were grouped by kind and inserted together where needed. Ribbons were floated and draped over everything like spun sugar. A garland of gold stars and shiny Christmas bulbs in pink, purple and rose completed the tree.

A CHRISTMAS TREE FOR THE GARDEN

As early as 1531, Christmas trees were brought into European homes. In the early years they were not decorated. Later, apples were hung on the trees, and in 1755 it was recorded that gilded potatoes, apples and other fruits were added. If you stop to think

Washed by the golden light of twilight, this Christmas tree, made entirely from dried flowers, sparkles.

A live evergreen tree planted in a fiberglass container is surrounded
by small poinsettia and ivy plants and decorated for Christmas
with dried flowers, lights and ribbons; later it will be planted outdoors
in the garden.

about it, it's a pretty strange custom to bring a tree inside and decorate it. But I'm glad someone thought of it, because it makes winter indoors much cheerier.

Some years I purchase a live evergreen to use as a Christmas tree. Later, when the weather warms, it can be planted in a permanent spot in the garden. If the tree is planted temporarily in a container like the white fiberglass one pictured at the left, it is easily moved indoors without causing a mess. After Christmas it can be moved back outside and left in the container until the weather is warm enough to dig a hole for planting. I have done it for years without ever losing an evergreen. They seem to adapt more easily than other plants to abrupt changes in temperatures.

Last Christmas I placed small pots of dwarf poinsettias with small-leaved, variegated ivy around the base to hide the soil. The tree was decorated with small, dried nosegays of red celosia surrounded by white baby's breath. The Christmas tree lights are battery operated and smaller than the plug-in varieties. The batteries can be hidden at the base of the tree, under the ivy, eliminating the need for an outlet and a draping cord. Ribbons, some with thin wire at their edges, softly curve and ripple as they stream down and around the tree.

Old-fashioned Christmas for the Birds

Decorate your Christmas tree with cranberry and popcorn garlands and, after Christmas, give these treats to the birds. Or decorate an outdoor tree early and give the birds a Christmas dinner. Welcome and encourage birds to stay in the garden all winter, to keep the garden lively, and all summer, because they help control the insects.

A good project to undertake with the kids is the old-fashioned stringing of cranberries and popcorn. Use lengths of less then four feet for your popcorn and cranberries; longer ones will break from the weight. An old-fashioned Christmas is an opportunity for the family to work together.

Individual pinecones, filled with peanut butter and rolled in birdseed, can be hung on an outdoor tree. I am told that raccoons love peanut butter and will come from miles around to get it, but they didn't attack my tree. Give the birds a little time to find the tree. If you have been feeding them all year you can expect them to find your tree in an hour or two, but if you are just beginning, give the birds a few days to discover it.

Cranberries, pinecones coated with peanut butter and sprinkled with birdseed, and popcorn make a perfect Christmas tree for the birds.

*Swags designed by
Peter Stevens
hang from sconces
on either side of a
fireplace.*

DECK THE HALLS

In ancient times evergreens, flourishing in winter, were believed to
have almost mystical powers. We can take advantage of all of the
evergreen plants from the shiny-smooth broadleafs to the more traditional prickly spruce, firs and pines, and combine them in winter
decorations. Rich effects are achieved by blending the textures and
colors from the large, smooth shades of dark-green rosettes of rhododendron leaves with the spiny sprigs of holly, the soft piles of
fir, draped golden cedar and bristled blue juniper. Additional color
can be added with the many berries still available: holly, barberry,
rose hips, juniper and winterberry, to name a few. The front hall
is welcoming when the banisters are wrapped with pine garlands
and ribbons, punctuated by groups of red globe amaranth—a sim-
pler but no less elegant approach is to bunch bare branches with
evergreens in the center of the banister. The sculptural branches of
winterberry with their scarlet-red balls are a natural holiday decoration for indoors. They are long-lasting and attractive with or without
ornaments on their branches.

A simple but elegant dressing for a staircase is bare branches bunched with evergreens in the center of the banister.

A close-up of an old-fashioned banister decoration.

The front hall is especially
welcoming when the
banisters are wrapped with
pine garlands and ribbons,
and punctuated by groups of
red gomphrena.

The sculptural branches of
winterberry with their
scarlet red balls are a
natural holiday decoration.

Other interesting evergreens to consider are andromeda, arborvitae, cedar, false cypress, leucothoe, euonymus, boxwood, bergenia and mountain laurel. The greens that hold their needles or leaves the longest are yew, cedar, fir, arborvitae, pine laurel, rhododendron, pittosporum, evergreen magnolia and evergreen holly.

It is easy to buy a ready-made wreath to use as a base and then wire on many different evergreens and berries from your garden to personalize your wreath. Or wire different greens onto a rope, which is easy to hang or drape. Because only one side of a garland was to be displayed, designer Peter Stevens laid a rope on a table, arranged the branches of boxwood and juniper on top of it and wired them in place down the length of rope. He attached a red ribbon to the top.

The ambitious can fashion a Christmas tree out of mixed greens—variegated holly, juniper and cedar, enhanced by bare birch twigs. It then needs only golden ribbons for decoration. Peter Stevens built the base of his tree with blocks of floral foam, making a pyramid the way a child would use building blocks. If it is built on a round tray, it will be easy to move and the tray will protect the table from the wet floral foam. The floral foam was not trimmed or cut to any shape and the blocks were piled on a base of three blocks, then two, and finally one at the top. The finished size will be almost twice as big as the floral foam base. The flat block on top will hold the terminal branch, which stands straight up to give the tree its conical shape. The blocks are held together by two long bamboo sticks going through the center of the floral foam blocks and several shorter bamboo sticks angling through the blocks. The finished construction is wrapped in chicken wire, which will help hold the branches. The branches are added one variety at a time, and the tree takes shape with fuller branches at the bottom and shorter ones at the top. If the construction is on a tray placed on a lazy Susan, it will be easier to turn and balance all sides as branches are added. If the tree is stationary it is important to continue to walk around the construction to add more branches where needed. The greens will stay fresh for several weeks if they are misted often, and if floral foam is kept moist, but even when they start to crinkle and dry they are attractive.

This Christmas tree is made of mixed greens and dried branches and is decorated with ribbons.

You can use the artificial trees decorated with dried flowers, which you will see in floral and gift shops, as inspiration for your own designs. This tree combines miniature wrapped presents, thin ribbons, white statice, rosebuds, berries and dried leaves. Its stand is hidden by wide loops of pink ribbon.

INDIVIDUAL ORNAMENTS WITH RIBBONS AND DRIED FLOWERS

Plain glass ornaments can be made into special gifts for a tree-trimming party by gluing dried flowers at the top and adding a decorative ribbon. If you prefer, use them as party favors to decorate your dinner table. Keep them from rolling around the table by placing them on curtain rings or flat, star-shaped napkin holders.

"There is no season such delight can bring
As summer, autumn, winter, and the spring."
—William Brown

A TOPIARY OF FRESH GREENS

Creating vignettes or personal still lifes that entertain and beautify a table can be a way to celebrate your family. Each of the figures in the scene on page 146 represents a member of our family, including our dog. The topiary tree is made with pieces of holly with their berries pressed into a floral-foam ball wrapped in chicken wire, which sits on top of a branch poked into a pot of ivy. The apples are held in place with flower picks.

The same ball of floral foam was reused in February to create a topiary of the year's first flowers. This time the branch was poked into a terra-cotta pot filled with floral foam. For a sturdier construction that can be reused, a branch can be held in place with a few inches of plaster at the bottom of the pot and covered with a few inches of floral foam to hold the greens. In this arrangement, I covered the ball with pachysandra and carefully pressed in the flowers of *Helleborus niger* and *Helleborus orientalis*, crocuses and double-flowered snowdrops. The base was decorated with the unopened buds of *Nadina*, several varieties of witch hazel and the burgundy branches of *Leucothoe*.

THE SCENT OF CHRISTMAS

The jar of potpourri you collected in the summer can reflect the changing seasons. Small sprigs of fresh pine, juniper, a smattering of cloves, allspice and cinnamon are the fragrances of Christmas. I like to break sticks of cinnamon into three- to four-inch pieces, to release their fragrance. Later, when the potpourri needs refreshing, break the sticks again. A few sprinkles of powdered cinnamon or allspice can also be added, but I think it makes the whole mixture look dusty so I put it in the bottom of the container for fragrance and don't mix it. Nestle in small pinecones for a wintry appearance and you've put Christmas in your potpourri. Essential oil of pine is also available for a stronger fragrance.

Left: A topiary of fresh holly, decorated with ribbons and apples, is placed in a houseplant of ivy.

This topiary was made in February of greens and the year's first flowers found in a northern garden still covered by snow.

WINTER CANDLE CUP

For the candle cup shown on page 150, everything was picked from the garden in late December after a snowfall, an ice storm, and a month of prolonged freezing temperatures—an unusual winter in our part of the country. I learned an important lesson: Continue to look in the garden in winter and never assume there is nothing to pick and bring in until April.

To make this candle cup, first completely cover the floral foam with inkberry to hide any tape or floral foam. Add one variety of plant at a time to balance the arrangement, aiming for subtle colorations and exploring the richness of textures. Add *Nadina* twigs with sprays of berries attached. The berries from the *Nadina* used here were uneaten by the birds and still holding well, not soft or decaying as were other berries in the garden. The cold weather tips their green leaves with red. Rose hips are a good alternative. Next add five sprigs of mountain laurel, with their unopened, nodding flower buds, and then a few sprigs of variegated euonymus. To finish, I picked flowering maple (*Abutilon*) flowers from a houseplant I've had for several years. It winters over in a sun room and summers in the garden, blooming almost constantly.

Another candle cup with a casual country feeling was designed and decorated by designer J. Barry Ferguson in March, with broad burgundy leaves from *Bergenia*, narrow drooping stems of variegated *Euonymus*, strands of ribbon grass, narrow burgundy leaves of *Leucothoe*, the marbled leaves of cyclamen and small-leaved ivy.

Go for a walk around your neighborhood, a nearby park or down a country road, where the abundance of nature reveals what you may not have imagined. Take pleasure in the walk, always more enjoyable with a purpose. Look for different textures, shapes and shades of green. Compare short and tall grasses, broad and narrow

The winter garden provided the variegated euonymus, Nadina and
mountain laurel that decorate the base of this candle cup. The
flowers were cut from a flowering maple houseplant (Abutilon species).

leaves, short- and long-needled evergreens, varicolored berries, the richly different shades of brown of nuts, acorns, pinecones and seedpods. Add a little imagination and put them together, to beautify the indoors and to blend with the kaleidoscope of changing seasons outdoors. A garden at all times, even in winter, is a world of limitless beauty and endless ideas.

PLANTS FOR WINTER ARRANGEMENTS

Bergenia: It holds its broad, red leaves all winter and flowers in the early spring.

Euonymus: All different types of *Euonymus* are good for winter arrangements. There are upright shrubs and groundcovers in plain, deep green or with gold or silver streaks.

Hardy cyclamen: Buy only from nurseries that grow it from seed; do not collect it from the wild, where it is endangered. Cyclamen has miniature nodding flowers, similar to those of the florist's cyclamen, in soft pink colors, reaching several inches above marbled, two- to three-inch rounded leaves. They bloom in late fall, but the leaves are wonderful in arrangements all winter (see the wreath on page 120).

Helleborus niger *and* H. orientalis: Commonly known as the Christmas rose and the Lenten rose, they bloom in midwinter.

Leucothoe *species*: These evergreens have oval, flat, leathery leaves (2½ to 4½ inches long) held on arching, spreading branches.

Liriope: There are many different varieties with striped silver or gold grasslike foliage as well as plain dark green. They hold their berries well into winter. Both the leaves and the berries can be picked for arrangements.

Myrtle: Myrtle is a garden workhorse, always dependable and available in winter to add green, delicate trailing leaves to an arrangement.

A Christmas bouquet combines a mixture of evergreens from the garden with bright red florist's flowers and includes: red amaryllis, parrot tulips, blue juniper berries, Japanese euonymus, holly, red rose hips and blue spruce.

Mountain laurel: They set their buds in the fall and hold them all winter before opening in the spring.

Nadina: Their green leaves slowly change to red, starting at the tips and creeping up the leaves as the weather gets colder, brightening a room at any time. The berries hold their color and plumpness for several months.

Pachysandra: Solid green or silver-edged varieties can be picked all winter.

Viola *'Princess Blue'*: This is a long-blooming and very early violet that I have picked in late February. It blooms from seed in approximately three months, even on a sunny windowsill.

Winterberry: A deciduous holly, winterberry's beauty shines brightest after frost strips the branches of their leaves to reveal multitudes of brilliant, cherry-red berries.

Witch hazel: There are many varieties with yellow or orange fragrant blooms in November and February. *Hamamelis* 'Arnold Promise' is a favorite for yellow, fragrant February blooms.

FLOWERING SHRUBS AND TREES FOR FORCING INDOORS

Forcing is the art of giving Mother Nature a gentle push, chiding her for keeping us indoors so long. It is a method of bringing flowers to bloom in advance of their natural cycle. Some flowering shrubs form their flower buds on old branches the summer or fall before they bloom. The buds are tightly bound to protect themselves from the ravages of winter and, depending on their bloom time, they gradually unwind and open as the weather warms. Fooling the buds into believing it is time to awaken from their winter nap is a simple trick. After January first, branches of such early-blooming shrubs as forsythia and witch hazel can be brought indoors to bloom. It is best to cut them when temperatures are above freezing and they are not covered with ice. If you must cut on a cold day, submerge the branches in a cool-water bath for several hours to gently thaw them out before placing them in warm water. When cutting, check for a branch with plump buds and cut it on a slant with a clean, sharp knife above a node (where a leaf is attached to the stem) or at the base of a branch. Bring your branches indoors and crush the bottom three inches of the branch with a hammer to expose a greater surface area of the fibers to the water, for longer-lasting blooms. Place the branches in warm, not hot, water for a half hour and then place in a dark, cool (50 degrees Fahrenheit) spot, letting them adjust to the warmer indoor temperatures for a few days before moving them into a warmer room. To keep bacteria from growing, you will need to change the water frequently, or add a water preservative. The buds don't need direct sunshine to open, but if you can give them a sunny window, their color will be stronger. Misting frequently or covering the branches with damp cheesecloth to simulate spring rains will speed the process. A clear plastic dry-cleaning bag, puffed with air to cover the branches and container, will act as a greenhouse, keeping moisture and heat inside.

There are many other flowering shrubs that are easily forced in early, mid- and late spring, when the branches could take many weeks to open. Generally, the closer to the normal bloom season the branches are cut, the faster they will open. I'm not in a big hurry to push the season, and I bring branches in only a few weeks before they are expected to bloom outdoors. When taking cuttings, remember to cut prudently several branches at different parts of the shrub where the look of the shrub will not be affected when it blooms naturally in the garden. Some shrubs, forsythia, for example, benefit from pruning every year and will quickly replace the branches you cut. Other shrubs, such as witch hazel, are slow growing

Flowering shrubs can be forced to bloom indoors earlier than they would naturally bloom outdoors.

and take two years for a new branch to bloom. I can't resist bringing in at least one fragrant branch of witch hazel in February when I need some indoor cheer. Usually I cut the branch into three pieces, fooling myself into thinking I have more. I make a small arrangement combining witch hazel with a background of greens.

Spring-blooming shrubs and trees for forcing include:

Azalea

Flowering almond

Flowering crab apple

Flowering dogwood

Flowering quince

Forsythia

Fothergilla

Fruit trees

Lilac

Magnolia

Ornamental cherry

Pussy willow

Even some trees can be forced, opening their beautiful foliage indoors. Try:

Beech

Birch

Hickory

Horse chestnut

Maple

Oak

"I'm still devoted to the garden . . . although an old man I am but a young gardener."
—Thomas Jefferson

FORCING INDOOR BULBS

When forcing daffodils or tulips, avoid the jack-in-the-box look of flowers popping out of the soil. Plant grass seed over the bulbs after their roots have formed and their tops are starting to grow. Grass grows quickly enough so that your bulbs will appear to be blooming in a dell of green. I once grew grass at the base of an Amaryllis, but in this case it looked ridiculous because it was so out of proportion with the tall stem of the Amaryllis. Alternatives are growing baby's tears around the rim of the pot, letting them drape over the edge, or placing Spanish or oak moss on top.

When forcing bulbs indoors, sow grass seed at their base to hide the soil. This rustic wooden planter complements the delicate lace doily.

CHAPTER FIVE

The Gardener's Cupboard

A gardener's cupboard stocked with a variety of staples for flower arrangements such as baskets, floral foam, vases and ribbons allows you to make arrangements on impulse. When flowers bloom unexpectedly early, guests are invited on short notice or an occasion arises for a gift to a friend, you'll be organized and prepared.

"How oft doth an emblem-bud silently tell
What language could never speak half so well!"
—*Romance of Nature*

PLANNING AHEAD

With an organized, thoughtful approach, time-consuming activities can be made simple. Flowers can be picked the morning or night before they must be arranged, and floral foam can be left sitting in water overnight. With everything ready to go, you simply arrange your flowers. It saves time on the day of your party, when every minute seems critical and everything takes longer than expected. Then, too, when you spread the activities over a longer time and plan ahead, you enjoy them more. Keep a cupboard of the staples you will use on a regular basis so you can bring spontaneity into your life. It heightens the fun and lessens the anxiety.

As in cooking, assemble the ingredients before you start. Once organized, everything is easier and a minimum of hassle brings more satisfying results. Without my garden cupboard and its staple of supplies, I would make a lot less use of my garden. It would be too frustrating. Here are some suggestions for items to keep on hand.

Assorted ribbons: From very thin for miniature arrangements to six inches wide for covering a large tin can to create a festive container.

Assorted vases, bowls, and containers: For arrangements of flowers and greens.

Baskets: All sizes including miniature ones.

Bucket: Nonmetal, for conditioning flowers.

Chicken wire: Can be scrunched in the neck of a large vase and taped in place to hold the flowers as they are arranged. It is also good for covering blocks of floral foam when making topiary forms.

Clear plastic self-adhesive paper: Useful to attach pressed flowers and leaves to glass, note cards or stationery.

Clear fishing line: To tie flowers and foliage to wreaths or to garlands (6- to 8-pound test is best).

Decorator moss: It is sold in bags and unrolls in sheets that can be cut to any desired size. Use to cover bare soil, or glue onto baskets or plastic containers. It has been harvested and air-dried to preserve its natural green color and beauty.

Green florist wire: To wrap around weak-stemmed or floppy flowers to help them hold their heads up, and to secure dried-flower heads.

Floral clay: A green sticky clay that can be broken easily into small pieces that are used to hold arrangements in place or, for example, candle cups in candle holders.

Floral foam: Green foam shapes that absorb water and hold flowers in place. The best-known brand name is Oasis.

Florist's tape: To hold arrangements in place in containers.

Flower-gathering basket: Low and long, to hold long-stemmed flowers lying down.

Flower preservatives: These contain the nutrients for conditioning flowers and are available from florists and garden centers. Cut flowers last longer when conditioned.

Plain gift cards: To decorate with fresh, dried or pressed flowers and attach to gifts.

Plastic flower tubes (water-pix): To hold single flowers or several thin-stemmed ones for arranging.

Plastic pots saved from purchased plants: Can be covered with ribbons or planted with leftover seedlings to grow and use as gifts later on.

Quick-dry liquid cement: Will take hold immediately, making it easy to glue dried flowers on baskets, Styrofoam or anything else.

Scissors and pruners: These need to be kept very sharp for cutting flower stems and branches.

Spanish moss (available in bags at nurseries and dime stores): It is harvested in long grayish-silver strands hung from trees in great masses. It grows naturally in the South. It can hide the soil in containers or at the base of flower arrangements and can be used as fillers on wreaths.

EXPRESS YOURSELF WITH FLOWERS

The gentle language of flowers is centuries old, existing long before the distant days of chivalry. It reflects feelings, caring and sentiment through the giving of flowers. In the course of being used by generation after generation it has taken some strange twists, depending on which book you use as your source and in which country the symbols originated. You will discover that the same plant can have different meanings in different places. (Basil symbolizes both hatred and love, depending on the source.)

If this were not complicated enough, there also exists a language based on how you actually hand flowers to friends. A flower handed upright symbolizes one thought, while upside down it symbolizes the opposite. A red rose symbolizes love even to the uninformed. But handed upright with its thorns attached it means "I fear, but I hope;" upside down, the meaning changes to "You must neither fear nor hope." When combined with other flowers it takes on new meaning having nothing to do with the singular meaning of each, because a bouquet means gallantry. Many mystery novels written in England require the reader to understand the significance of various flowers in order to solve the mystery!

While reading a century-old book on the language of flowers, I came across this tale:

> One day, said the poet Sadi, "I saw a rosebush surrounded by a tuft of grass." "What!" I cried. "Does that vile plant dare to place itself in the company of Roses?" I was about to tear the grass away, when it meekly addressed me, saying, "Spare me! I am not the Rose, it is true; but, from my perfume, anyone may know at least that I have lived with Roses." What fun to make a nosegay of roses surrounded by one of the wonderful ornamental grasses that are all the rage in America today and to give it to a friend along with a card explaining the story and saying, "There is everything to be gained by good company."

So what do we do with all of the confusing symbols of flowers? We pick what we like and discard the rest. Forget the symbols of flowers that represent unhappy, nasty and hateful sentiments. The world has enough of those, and flowers are not the proper vehicle to express them. As many of these flowers are beautiful, group them into bouquets for a gallant gesture.

For the shy or inarticulate, a note expressing the language of flowers can lend charm to reflect feelings of gratitude, friendship, love and comfort. I have chosen my favorites, but there are many more, and you will enjoy discovering them for yourself and adapting them to your way of life. Remember that simplicity and sincerity are also necessary ingredients.

Left: In the language of flowers, common ribbon grass surrounding aristocratic roses says "There is everything to be gained by good company."

Here are some of the most useful meanings.

American cowslip or shooting star—You are my angel
Buttercup—cheerfulness
Campanula—gratitude
Columbine—folly
Coreopsis—always cheerful
Crocus—pleasures of hope
Dahlia—My gratitude exceeds your care
Daisy—innocence
Flax—I am sensible of your kindness
Forget-me-not—forget me not
Gomphrena—unfading love
Hollyhock—fruitfulness
Honeysuckle—bonds of love
Ivy—friendship
Jonquil—Have pity on my passion (or desire)
Laurel—glory
Lilac—first emotion of love
Lily-of-the-valley—return of happiness
Lily—majesty
Mignonette—Your qualities surpass your charms
Myrtle—love
Pansy—Think of me
Phlox—proposal of love
Rose—beauty
Rosemary—your presence revives me
Sage—esteem
Sweet sultan—happiness
Tulip—declaration of love

Tie your note card with a ribbon and decorate it with a pressed herb or flower. For special celebrations, set a table personalizing each place card with a miniature arrangement or boutonniere and a thought for each guest. The flowers themselves act as symbols to express your caring. Because most people today are not familiar with what individual flowers symbolize, the place cards can explain the meaning for special events. A rose stripped of its thorns says, "There is everything to be hoped for," an expression appropriate for the college graduate, the new job, an approaching wedding or birth. Or, "This rose is for your beauty," "The laurel glories in your success," "Ivy, the symbol of true friends," and, "Rosemary, like your presence, revives me."

A bouquet of coreopsis could be accompanied by a note to say "Like you, a bouquet of coreopsis is always cheerful." A spring nosegay of pansies surrounded by myrtle could convey the sentiment "The myrtle expresses my love, the pansy my hope that you'll think of me." A note for a mixture of columbine and forget-me-nots might say "My friend the columbine says, 'This may be folly, but please forget me not.'" Let the language of flowers bring out your feelings.

CUTTING FLOWERS

There can never be too many flowers; in the words of Mae West, "Too much of a good thing is just wonderful." That's why my cutting garden expands yearly, and flowers can be seen moving out and mingling with herbs and vegetables.

Cutting gardens, freshly planted each spring so that they produce bouquets on demand all summer, were long a part of the venerable old hotels where the quality of service and ambiance was unquestionable. Today, you needn't go to the Ritz to find a delightfully fragrant little bouquet by your bedside or a handsome centerpiece on your dining room table that makes you feel pleasantly spoiled. The luxury of cut flowers is available to everyone, even if you have to buy a few to supplement the ones in your garden. Many American gardens are planned with an area reserved for flowers grown especially for cutting.

Gathering flowers from the garden is one of a gardener's great pleasures. You can arrange them for the living room, the dining room, guest room or wherever they will be enjoyed by family and friends. An especially nice feature to keep in mind with cutting flowers is that the more you cut, the more flowers your annuals produce. The supply is self-perpetuating.

I grow an annual flower garden to beautify an old wall. When the garden produces an abundance of flowers, I cut some to bring inside, but always take care to cut judiciously. I scatter the cuts to distribute the benefits of thinning and to avoid leaving noticeable bald spots in the garden. I also plant flowers for cutting purposes among my vegetables, and these I relentlessly strip of blossoms for our house and for giving to friends and neighbors. If you choose to do this, you can lay the garden out in easily accessible rows, mulch with black plastic between the rows, and if you don't like

Flowers from W. Atlee Burpee & Co.'s annual cutting garden de-
signed by Alice R. Ireys include orange cosmos 'Bright Lights',
pink cosmos 'Sensation', pink and purple pincushion flowers 'Giant
Imperial', and white and pink asters 'Burpeeana Extra Early'.

the appearance of the plastic, cover it with straw or grass. This is a strictly functional cutting garden.

When you begin planning the flowers you want to grow for cutting, include many that are fragrant. They will enhance your pleasure.

A Chinese bucket is filled with blooms from an August garden including zinnias, marigolds, pincushion flowers, blue salvias, plumed celosias, delphiniums and silver-edged pachysandras.

FRAGRANT ANNUALS FOR CUTTING

Common Name	Latin Name
Alyssum	*Alyssum*
Candytuft	*Iberis*
Flossflower	*Ageratum*
Flowering tobacco	*Nicotiana*
Heliotrope	*Heliotropium*
Knapweed	*Centaurea*
Marigold	*Tagetes*
Mignonette	*Reseda*
Moonflower	*Ipomoea alba*
Nasturtium	*Tropaeolum*
Pansy	*Viola* × *Wittrockiana*
Petunia	*Petunia*
Phlox	*Phlox*
Pincushion flower	*Scabiosa*
Pink	*Dianthus*
Pot marigold	*Calendula*
Scented geranium	*Pelargonium*
Snapdragon	*Antirrhinum*
Spider plant	*Cleome*
Stock	*Matthiola*
Sweet pea	*Lathyrus*
Thorn apple	*Datura*

FRAGRANT PERENNIALS FOR CUTTING

Common Name	Latin Name
Basket-of-gold	*Aurinia*
Catmint	*Nepeta*
Daylily (some varieties)	*Hemerocallis*
Double bouncing bet	*Saponaria officinalis*
Gas plant	*Dictamnus*
Honeysuckle (flowering vine)	*Lonicera*

FRAGRANT PERENNIALS FOR CUTTING (cont.)

Common Name	Latin Name
Peony	*Paeonia*
Pinks	*Dianthus*
Plantain lily 'Royal Standard'	*Hosta*
Primrose	*Primula*
Sage	*Salvia*
Sweet woodruff	*Galium odoratum*
Violet	*Viola*
Wormwood	*Artemisia*

BULBS, CORMS AND TUBERS

Common Name	Latin Name
Crocus	*Crocus*
Daffodil	*Narcissus*
Freesia	*Freesia*
Gladiola	*Gladiolus*
Glory-of-the-snow	*Chionodoxa*
Grape hyacinth	*Muscari*
Hyacinth	*Hyacinthus*
Iris	*Iris*
Lily	*Lilium*
Puschkinia	*Puschkinia*
Siberian squill	*Scilla siberica*
Snowdrop	*Galanthus*

FRAGRANT FLOWERING SHRUBS

Common Name	Latin Name
Butterfly bush	*Buddleia*
Daphne	*Daphne*
Flowering almond	*Prunus glandulosa*
Fothergilla	*Fothergilla*
Gardenia	*Gardenia*
Honeysuckle	*Lonicera fragrantissima*
Jasmine	*Jasminum*
Lilac	*Syringa*
St.-John's-wort	*Hypericum*
Summer-sweet	*Clethra*
Viburnum	*Viburnum*
Witch hazel	*Hamamelis*

CONDITIONING CUT FLOWERS

There is a proper way to cut and condition flowers to prolong their life, often helping them stay fresh two weeks or longer. Many of the flowers you see in florists' shops have been flown in from all over the country, as well as from Europe, South America and even the Far East. These flowers have been conditioned to allow them to be boxed and shipped out of water for a day or two. As a home gardener you can prolong the life of flowers with a few simple procedures borrowed from professional florists.

Use these guidelines:

The time to gather cut flowers is when the sun is low, in the morning or evening. Stems are apt to wilt quickly if cut in midday, when the sun is hot and the plants are losing water. If you must cut in the middle of the day, carry a clean bucket (not metal, because some flowers react badly to it) of warm water and immerse the stems as quickly as you cut them.

For most flowers, the time for cutting is when the buds are about half open. If buds are in a small cluster, cut some of them in flower but include unopened buds, which will become healthy blooms later, lengthening the lifetime of the bouquet. A few flowers, among them zinnias, marigolds, asters and dahlias, should be picked in full bloom, but these will last and continue to look good in their new surroundings.

Cut stems at an angle to allow a larger surface to absorb water. Cut the stems as long as possible without taking too many unopened buds. This will allow you more flexibility when arranging the flowers and protect the buds, which are tomorrow's flowers. Make the cut with clean, sharp scissors or a sharp knife. You don't want to crush or bruise the stems. If there are leaves at the bottom of the stem remove them; leaves left on the stem under water will decay and smell unpleasant. If you have cut the flowers in the garden and not put them directly into water, recut the stems after you bring them inside and before conditioning them. The bottoms of the stems begin to dry if left out of water for even a few minutes. Some experts recommend cutting the stem under water, but there is no evidence to prove that this is necessary. (The Japanese, known for their beautiful gardens and arrangements, follow traditional wisdom and believe in recutting flower stems under water because flowers belong to the element water, not air.)

The most effective steps for prolonging the blooming of your cut flowers are those taken early. You want the plants to absorb as much water as possible, and you can sometimes double the life of cut flowers by plunging them in warm water as soon as possible after they are picked. Some experts recommend that the temperature of the water be the same as the air to minimize the shock to the plants. They have been shocked enough by being cut. Remember, the emphasis is on warm. It's easy to think the opposite: You splash your face with cold water to stimulate and wake up your senses, but with flowers the opposite holds. Warmth stimulates, but cold slows down, the action within the plants.

After cutting and immersing the flowers in warm water, place them in a cool place for four to twelve hours to allow the stems to fill completely with water. The cool-air and warm-water combination conditions the flowers and extends their life as cut flowers. Recently a Dutch researcher compared the vase life of cut lilac sprays placed in varying depths of water, from two to eight inches deep. The results of the study after three days showed that the deeper the water, the greater the intake of water into the branches, and the longer the flowers lasted. This helps explain why flowers conditioned in water up to their "necks" last longer, even when subsequently placed in arrangements with shallow water.

Small packets of commercial preservatives are available from florists and nurseries. They prolong the life of cut flowers and are used by professional florists and flower growers. The packets contain beneficial chemicals as follows:

1. Sugar, in a form that can be used by the plant for quick energy.

2. Bacteria inhibitors that prevent the stems from clogging.

3. Acidic compounds that lower the alkalinity of the water and impede the growth of micro-organisms.

4. Metallic salts that help preserve the color of the flowers.

5. Respiratory inhibitors to lower the metabolic rate of the flowers.

Use the packets while conditioning the flowers and again later when arranging them. These preparations will keep your flowers healthy, blooming and holding their heads high. Although not as thoroughly beneficial as the commercial preservatives, a few drops of liquid

Flowers in individual vases can give a full look when flowers are few.

household bleach and a teaspoon of sugar will help, too. The bleach will do what it does for swimming pools: prevent fungus from growing (it will not harm the blossoms). The sugar will be quick-energy food, but don't use it without the bleach; used alone, it will speed up the growth of fungus.

If it is an especially hot day and your flowers look quite droopy when you bring them in from the garden, there is a quick fix. Immerse the ends of the flower stems one-fourth to one-half inch into boiling water for 30 seconds, while keeping their petals out of the rising steam. Then condition them in a cool place as explained previously. Often even the droopiest will be revived by this treatment.

Special attention: Dahlias, poppies, *Euphorbia* and other flowers that ooze a sticky liquid when cut need special care. This liquid will eventually coagulate and cause blockage in the stem, preventing them from absorbing water. By dipping the stem ends in boiling water or searing the ends with a match, you can prevent them from becoming clogged and extend their life as cut flowers.

ARRANGING FLOWERS

Your flower arrangements need not be elaborate and time-consuming. Float a single fragrant flower (try nasturtium, moonflower, gardenia, dahlia or dianthus) in a bowl. Put an individual, long-stemmed flower (cosmos, salvia or marigold) in a slim, tall vase or cut the stems short and place flowers individually in a series of miniature glass bottles and group them together on a table. Try a tightly packed arrangement of one type of flower where the flower itself is what catches your eye, not the container. Sometimes the flowers are even more effective if the leaves are stripped off and the focus is only on the flowers.

For that special occasion, when a larger arrangement in a basket or a vase is needed, there are many flower-arranging tools available to the home gardener. One is the floral foam Oasis—invaluable. It is available as bricks to cut and shape, candle cups (so you can surround your candles with a small bouquet) and rings for wreaths to hang or place on a table. Remember when working with floral foam to cut it with a sharp knife and at an angle, and that it will lose its ability to hold water if squeezed or compressed. Soak it thoroughly by floating it in water until it absorbs enough to sink and bubbles stop rising from it. This could take an hour or more. Don't force the floral foam under water, or it may absorb water on all four sides but trap air in the middle—right where the stems of your flowers will be. For longer life you can add a flower life-extending solution to the water. Use a green floral tape to tape the wet floral foam to your container, whether it be a candle cup, bowl or plastic liner for the inside of a basket. The best arrangements hide the floral foam with greens or moss before adding flowers. If you are using only flowers, use them abundantly. After you've finished, turn the arrangement to be sure all tape and floral foam are covered.

No matter what type of arrangement you decide on, there are a few simple rules that will extend the life of your flowers. Be sure the container you use is very clean. If you're using commercial preservative, add more warm water to the container daily to replace what is lost through evaporation. If not using preservative, discard the old water and refill with fresh warm water every day to prevent the build-up of fungus. Fungus and bacteria that grow in water not only smell bad after a few days but can stain the inside of the containers holding the arrangements, and these stains can be diffi-

A candle cup filled with floral foam is ready to be decorated.

cult to remove conventionally with soap and water. (The Brooklyn Botanic Garden reports that a tea-leaves-and-vinegar concoction will quickly remove stains. Mix a few tablespoons of loose tea leaves in a cup or more of white vinegar and swish it around inside the stained container until the stain is gone.) Keep the arrangement out of direct sunlight and drafts. You can prepare an arrangement a day or two ahead for a special occasion if you condition the flowers (see page 174). Flowers are further helped if stored in a cool place (a refrigerator, if you have room, or a basement) until needed.

Conditioned flowers, bunched and tied with a ribbon or lace, can simply be placed flat on a tabletop. After conditioning (six hours in water), they will be able to survive several hours or even a day or longer without water. Cornflowers (*Centaurea Cyanus*) can last for four days or longer out of water, looking all the while as though they have just been picked.

This completed candle cup is decorated with red and yellow tulips, variegated ivy and mountain laurel.

A set of floral-foam rings.

Roses and ivy cover a floral-foam ring in a romantic arrangement.

BIBLIOGRAPHY

Bubel, Nancy Wilkes. *The Adventurous Gardener*. Boston: David R. Godine, Publisher, 1979.

Coats, Alice M. *Flowers and Their Histories*. New York, Toronto, London: Pitman Publishing Corporation, 1956.

Cowles, Fleur. *Flower Decorations*. New York: Villard Books, 1985.

Creasy, Rosalind. *Cooking from the Garden*. San Francisco: Sierra Club Books, 1988.

Dickinson, Emily. *The Complete Poems of Emily Dickinson*. Edited by Thomas H. Johnson. Boston, Toronto, London: Little Brown and Company, 1960.

Everett, Thomas H. *The New York Botanical Garden Illustrated Encyclopedia of Horticulture*. New York: Garland Publishing, 1981.

Ferguson, J. Barry, and Tom Cowan. *Living with Flowers*. New York: Rizzoli International Publications, 1990.

Left: Goldenrod is much maligned. It doesn't cause allergies. Here it is the center of an arrangement surrounded by gaillardia, cosmos 'Bright Lights' and blue salvia, with the vine love-in-a-puff trailing out of the basket and over the side.

Fox, Frances Margaret. *Flowers and Their Travels*. Bridgeport, Conn.: The Bobbs-Merrill Company, 1936.

Hillier, Malcolm. *Decorating with Dried Flowers*. New York: Crown Publishers, Inc., 1987.

Ohrbach, Barbara Milo. *A Bouquet of Flowers*. New York: Clarkson N. Potter, Inc/Publishers, 1990.

Otis, Denise, Ronaldo Maia and Ernst Beadle. *Decorating with Flowers*. New York: Harry N. Abrams, Inc., Publishers, 1978.

Tyas, Robert, M.A., LL.D., F.R.B.S. *The Language of Flowers*. New York: George Routledge and Sons, 1894.

Verey, Rosemary. *The Scented Garden*. New York: Random House, 1981.

Waugh, Dorothy. *A Handbook of Christmas Decorations*. New York: The Macmillan Company, 1958.

Wyman, Donald. *Wyman's Gardening Encyclopedia*. New York: Macmillan, 1986.

Index